Figs, Dates, Laurel, and Myrrh

Figs, Dates, Laurel, and Myrrh

Plants of the Bible and the Quran

LYTTON JOHN MUSSELMAN

foreword by
GARRISON KEILLOR

TIMBER PRESS

Frontispiece: A Sudanese man using a board from acacia to copy verses from a collection of praises. His inkpot, on his right, contains a mixture of charcoal, gum arabic, and other products. After the board is filled, the writing is washed off so the board can be used again.

Facts stated in this book are to the best of the author's knowledge true, but the author and publisher can take no responsibility for the misidentification of plants by the users of this book nor for any illness that might result from their consumption. If there is any doubt whatsoever about the identity or edibility of a plant, do not eat it.

Photographs are by the author unless otherwise indicated.

Published in 2007 by
Timber Press, Inc.
The Haseltine Building
133 S.W. Second Avenue, Suite 450
Portland, Oregon 97204-3527, U.S.A.
www.timberpress.com

For contact information regarding editorial, marketing, sales, and distribution in the United Kingdom, see www.timberpress.co.uk.

Printed in China

Library of Congress Cataloging-in-Publication Data

Musselman, Lytton J.
 Figs, dates, laurel, and myrrh: plants of the Bible and the Quran/Lytton John Musselman; foreword by Garrison Keillor.
  p. cm.
 Includes bibliographical references and index.
 ISBN-13: 978-0-88192-855-6
 1. Plants in the Bible. 2. Plants in the Koran. I. Title.
 BS665.M87 2007
 220.8′58—dc22   2007019025

A catalog record for this book is also available from
the British Library.

Solo Deo Gloria

Contents

Foreword

I N THE BIBLE PICTURE BOOKS of my childhood, the Holy Land was an arid plain with some mountains in the distance. Men in turbans and robes rode their grim-faced camels toward an oasis of palm trees. Here and there, men toiled in vineyards, and when it was time for Jesus to be crucified, he went to the Mount of Olives. But mostly scripture was without much vegetation, so far as our picture books were concerned. There were the green pastures, of course, and the lilies, and the Song of Solomon was dripping with plants and fervid feeling and *your neck is like a tower of David and your breasts like two small rabbits* and references to thighs, but by and large, Canaan did not seem so pleasant or promising. In Bethlehem and Jerusalem and Nazareth, houses were jammed in tight on narrow streets, no lawns or shrubs, so unlike 14th Avenue South in Minneapolis where I attended Sunday School at the Grace & Truth Gospel Hall, where stately elms made a solid canopy over the pavement and lush grass grew and nearby was Powderhorn Park where we tossed a softball around between Bible Reading at 3 p.m. and Gospel Meeting at 7:30.

We were Plymouth Brethren and we were rather arid ourselves, if the truth be told, more like cactuses than fruit trees. Our bunch was a little band of 50 Christians who stuck to their guns though reduced by painful schisms and dominated by an alpha male, an engineer, a stubborn German who ran a tight ship. They clung to their belief in the literal truth of scripture, the priesthood of all believers, the silence of women, services conducted according to the leading of the Spirit,

Apricot tree laden
with fruit in June, near
Deir Attaya, Syria

communion reserved for those in tight agreement on doctrine—and every year there were more empty seats in their midst. The young people kept defecting, going over the wall to the Baptists and Presbyterians, trying to escape that aridness, that sense of decline in the air. The Brethren accepted decline as more or less inevitable, even as a sign of their own faithfulness. (Many are called, but few are chosen.) They did not expect showers of blessing or a great flowering or a magnificent harvest, not here, not in this life. They hunkered in the dust and prayed for endurance.

Scripture speaks of pastures and vineyards and wheat fields but I did not envision these in my Christian imagination. The idea of the gospel as a seed was lost on me. (It was more like a precious jewel that had been given to us and that we kept locked in a box.) Mine was an indoor faith, under a roof, with many empty seats and a dogged orthodoxy that was more like a fortress than a garden. Our pope was J. N. Darby, the father of the Brethren movement, who had been dead for years and so his dicta could not be questioned. He was a separatist and so we were separated too. We were like a tiny ghetto.

My father probably felt otherwise about all of this, he being a farm boy and a passionate gardener. We lived on an acre lot north of Minneapolis along the Mississippi River and grew tomatoes, beans, corn, cucumbers, melons, strawberries, spinach, squash, and peas to feed six growing children. I did not inherit his love of plants and I had a habit of sneaking away from garden chores and hiding in a ravine, a lovely overgrown creek bed, and lounging around under the sumac and red oaks and imagining myself a Union spy behind Confederate lines. The trees themselves did not interest me. They were only a backdrop. I have maintained my ignorance of botany to the present day, and that is why Lytton Musselman asked me to write a foreword: he knew it was the only way to get me to read the book.

Friend Musselman's book is shocking to me. Here is a distinguished American botanist with years of research experience in the Middle East pointing at the picture book I still carry in my mind and saying,

"It was not an apple that Eve gave to Adam. It may have been an apricot. It sure was not an apple." This is a jolt to an old believer like me. I can accept that the lilies ("Consider the lilies of the field") may have been anemones and that the tree Zaccheus climbed was not our sycamore and that the rose of Sharon may have been a gladiolus or that the willows they hung their harps in may have been poplars. Nor does it trouble me that the mustard seed of the parable might have been arugula. "Except your faith be like unto the arugula"—that is going to go over well with the Episcopalians.

Until I read Musselman's book, I did not know what myrrh is. I am sixty-four and a college graduate but if a child had asked me, "What is myrrh?" I would have been forced to lie. "The name, my dear, comes from polymer, it was an early plastic formed as a byproduct when they burned rubber plants, and it was considered quite precious, and that's why the Wise Men brought it as a gift for the Christ Child, so He could form it into a ball in his tiny hand and bounce it on the floor." Wrong. It is the dried resin of several species of shrubs in the genus *Commiphora*. You get this resin by squeezing *commas* and if you sniff it you become *euphoric*.

Balm of Gilead is likewise a resin, from the terebinth tree, not just a line in a hymn. I love a fact like this, though terebinth trees have never loomed large in my life, nor has saffron. Nonetheless it is good to know that 75,000 saffron flowers are needed to produce the threads to make one pound (454 grams) of the spice. "Your thighs shelter a paradise of pomegranates with rare spices," sang Solomon, and one of those spices was saffron. (Cinnamon and aloe too. Check it out the next time you're in the vicinity of a thigh.)

And rue is a sort of citrus plant, yellow, used some places to make tea. Professor Musselman notes, "Whether or not rue should be ingested is debatable." I myself do not intend to debate this point. I am going on a strict non-rue diet from here on.

"The translators of the influential King James Version had little firsthand knowledge of plants of the Middle East," says our teacher patiently. (One wonders what *else* did they have little firsthand knowledge of—women? tolerance? humor?) He corrects them gently, but his great contribution is simply to green up the Book for those of us who always imagined it to be like the Great Salt Flats. This is a great accomplishment, though I am still bothered by the apple/apricot business. After a lifetime of biting into apples and imagining them to be forbidden fruit and therefore all the more delicious, I find it hard to transfer this to a smaller fruit. I have no trouble with Darwin's theory at all, but the idea of the tree of knowledge being an apricot tree—this is a matter for further prayer, Brother Musselman. Eat an apple and think about this some more.

GARRISON KEILLOR
Saint Paul

Mature olive tree on Mount of Olives, Jerusalem. Tour guides sometimes refer to these trees as having been there in the time of Christ. While olives may live hundreds of years, none are known to be two thousand years old.

Preface

I LOVE PLANTS. I love the Bible. And living and working in several Arab countries has given me a deep appreciation of Islamic culture and the Quran. This book reflects these passions and my desire to share and to celebrate the lore of plants and their uses as expressed in the Bible and the Quran—whether the plants are obscure, noxious, utilitarian, or cultic species. Indeed, the Divine takes a celebratory tone when discussing plants in these holy books. From the Bible: "I give every green plant for food. And it was so. God saw all that he had made, and it was very good" (Genesis 1:30b–31a, NIV). And from the Quran: "He positioned the earth for all the creatures: There are fruits of all kinds on it, and date-palms with their clusters sheathed, grain—with husk, and fragrant grasses" (Sura 55:10–12, Ali), which are "favors of your Lord."

My objectives are twofold: to help readers of the scriptures better understand the ecologic and cultural factors that led to various plants' inclusion in holy writ, and to provide insights regarding the plants themselves, their diversity of form, color, smell, and use.

When I started this project more than 20 years ago, I had a straight-forward goal: to study every plant mentioned in the Bible and the Quran growing in nature; to learn how local people still use these plants today; to compare current uses with how people used these plants in ancient times; to establish what controversies, past and present, surround these plants' identities; and, generally, to assimilate all I could about this remarkable assemblage of plants. Alas, I have not yet

Date palm in a church mosaic from the Byzantine era in Medaba, Jordan. The use of palm tree as an icon is widespread including on the currency of several countries.

seen *Aquilaria* (aloeswood) or *Nardostachys* (spikenard, or nard) in the field. But I have been blessed with seeing all the others.

Even if I had been able to experience all plants clearly identified in both holy books, it would not be possible to include all those plants in this study because some are figurative and have no true botanical counterpart. For example, consider two trees. The Quran mentions the terrible tree of Hell, *zaqqum*, which has fruits like devils' heads that when consumed burn your stomach: "Is this not a better welcome than the zaqqum tree? We have made this tree a scourge for the unjust. It grows in the nethermost part of Hell, bearing fruit like devils' heads: on it they shall feed, and with it they shall cram their bellies, together with draughts of scalding water. Then to Hell shall they return" (Sura 37:62–68, Dawood). *Zaqqum* is also found in Sura 44:43–44 and Sura 56:51–55. Trying to link this tree with an actual plant is both botanically and theologically untenable. Similarly, the tree of life mentioned in the last book of the Bible, Revelation 22:14, is also figurative: "Blessed are those who will have washed their robes clean, so that they will have the right to feed on the tree of life and can come through the gates into the city" (NJB). This passage presents an image of something supernatural with the tree as a literary device.

Relegating these trees to the numinous is reasonable as is the burning bush in the story of Moses: "The angel of Yahweh appeared to him in a flame blazing from the middle of a bush. Moses looked; there was the bush blazing, the bush was not being burnt up" (Exodus 3:2, NJB). I place these references in the realm of supernatural events. Much has been written on the divine provision in the desert—manna—by scholars of both the Bible and the Quran (Moldenke and Moldenke 1952; Zohary 1982; Farooqi 2003). Likewise, another plant with miraculous properties, in this case maturing in a single day, was translated as "gourd" in the story of Jonah in both the Quran, "We made a gourd tree grow over him" (Sura 37:146, Ali); and the Bible, "And the lord God prepared a gourd, and made it to come up over Jonah, that it might be a shadow over his head, to deliver him from his grief. So Jonah was exceeding glad of the gourd" (Jonah 4:6, KJV, though many other translations do not use "gourd" in this verse). Since the plant discussed in the Bible germinated and grew extensively within a single day, it was clearly not a garden-variety gourd (or, as some translators suggest, castor bean). Accepting the preternatural is part of my theological foundation, though as an ethnobotanist I would love to understand the cultural influences that shaped the literary images in the holy scriptures, but that is beyond the scope of this project.

A second category of plants was excluded from this study. General terms like "grass," "trees," "grains," "fruits," "sweet smelling plant," and "bitter plant" defy precise identity. The use of such imprecise terms in scripture was no doubt deliberate. There are numerous examples of obscure plants in both the Quran and the Bible, and humility is needed when trying to identify them.

Many authors over the centuries have been drawn to expatiate on the attractive topic of Bible plants. No books on the topic have appeared during the past decade, however, and over this period much has been learned about ancient uses. Plants of the Quran have likewise not received much attention, though that literature is less accessible to English speakers for language reasons. Many plants and their uses are mentioned in the Hadith (sayings of the Prophet Mohammad), the Mishnah of Judaism, and many writings of the Christian Church. While fascinating, these topics are beyond the scope of this work. I hope this volume will encourage investigation of plants in these pseudepigrapha, with resultant integration of information among these three religions germinated in the soil of western Asia. In short, I am restricting my coverage to plants found in the Quran, the Old Testament (including the Apochrypha), and the New Testament. Writing about the plants in both sacred volumes in one book is logical and synergistic for botanical and theological reasons but, to my knowledge, has not been attempted before.

I have written about the plants of the Quran with a sense of inadequacy. The number of well-defined plants in the Quran are about onequarter those of the Bible. And, with rare exceptions, they are the same plants with the same uses. Yet to my Muslim family members, friends, colleagues, and students, I ask your grace and understanding in my attempt to bring the plants of the two holy codices under one cover. I have experienced most of the plants of the Quran, but I do not have nearly the same knowledge of their lore as I do for plants of the Old and New Testaments of the Bible.

Writing with any authority on plants of the Bible and the Quran requires a familiarity with both the flora and the texts. Ideally the writer should have training in theology, textual criticism, as well as firsthand knowledge of the plants of the region. The only person I know who met the criteria is George Edward Post, who wrote the first modern flora of the Middle East (Post 1896; Dinsmore 1932; Musselman 2006). His impact on Bible plant knowledge through his entries in Bible dictionaries still in print has not yet been carefully considered, and a critical view of the interplay of botany and the sacred texts has seldom been argued.

One example is concern about solid text criticism by Trever (1959), who pointed out how professional botanists (for example, Moldenke and Moldenke 1952) misunderstood the literary style of Bible texts. While bemoaning this lack of light, Trever cites an example of *Juniperus oxycedrus*, "shrubs growing among rocky crags of the desert wastes" (Trever 1959), apparently unaware that *J. oxycedrus* is not a desert plant.

Nor are such botanical misrepresentations restricted to the Bible. In the Ali translation of the Quran, the *zaqqum*, the tree of Hell, is described as having "spathes . . . like the prickly pear" (Sura 37:65, Ali). Prickly pear is the accepted common name of *Opuntia*, a genus of cactus widely planted in western Asia (and elsewhere) but native to the New World and unknown to the ancients in the days of the Prophet.

In addition to solid plant science and careful exegesis, a third approach is needed—urgently—as traditional societies are recast from agrarian to urban. That is ethnobotany, the study of how people and societies use plants, especially traditional uses of plants. Ethnobotany has been a major concern of mine, and I have tried to learn as much from the indigenous farmers and village inhabitants as possible in the different countries where I have studied.

Acknowledgments

HOW DO I BEGIN TO THANK the myriad people on four continents who have taught me so much during the past two decades? Generously.

I gratefully acknowledge three Fulbright awards: the first at the University of Khartoum in 1982–1984, the second at An Najah University in 1986–1987, and the third at the University of Jordan in 1998–1999. In addition to agricultural research, contacts and friendships resulting from these opportunities have greatly enriched my understanding of Bible plants in their natural settings, and they have graced me and my family in so many other ways.

While abroad, I was privileged to work with several national and international organizations. Professors Abraham Fahn and Clara Heyne of the Hebrew University introduced me to the flora. It was a pleasure to work for several summers with Jordan's Royal Society for the Conservation of Nature and to visit their spectacular preserves. In 2002–2004 I had the privilege to work with the agrobiodiversity program hosted by the International Center for Agricultural Research in the Dry Areas (ICARDA) and their programs in the Palestinian Territories, Lebanon, and Syria; Ahmed Amri helped and supported me in this project. A royal thank you to Her Majesty Queen Rania al-Abdullah of Jordan for the commission to write on wildflowers in her country (Musselman 2000).

In 2001, I was a visiting professor at Aleppo University and in 2002 at the American University of Beirut. In both of these places I received innumerable kindnesses and help. Worthy of special note are Professors Majd Jamal, Fawaz Azmeh, and Ibtasam Hamad of Damascus University, who arranged for visits to so many natural areas to study plants and expended so much time and hospitality in assisting me. Professor

Jamal, now Director General of the General Direction of Scientific
Research, Ministry of Agriculture for Syria, continues to build relationships between plant scientists in our two countries.

In addition, I would have learned little that is new about plants of
the two holy books without firsthand interaction with the farmers and
shepherds who continue the ancient uses of many of the plants.

The genesis of this project occurred in my early childhood because
of high value placed in my home on the Bible's teachings. This experience was later augmented when I lived in many of the countries written about in the scriptures. But the idea of this book began with Doug
Hayhoe, who encouraged me long ago to begin this study while at a
most unbiblical setting—the north woods of Canada. And that led to
other projects. Henk Medema thoughtfully arranged for translation of
some of my early work into Dutch; it appeared in two booklets (Musselman and Medema 1993 and 1993a). I have incorporated some of his
exegesis on mustard and hyssop. Dean Ohlman of Radio Bible Class
taught me the importance of trees in the Bible and, by extension, the
imagery of trees in other religious writings. Most recently, without
the counsel and assistance of the folks at Timber Press, I would not
have completed this book.

Nigel Hepper, formerly of the Royal Botanic Gardens, Kew, and
author of several books on Bible plants, has been a botanical and Bible
friend for more than three decades. He read several drafts of this book
and his valuable criticisms have been carefully weighed. To Garrison Keillor, my appreciation for writing a foreword. Both of us spring
from the same Plymouth Brethren (Grant-Booth Meeting) with its
high value on Bible knowledge, reflected in Keillor's frequent references to the Bible in his programs and writings. Professor M. H.
Farooqi, whose books on plants in Islam are the most widely appreciated in English, graciously read sections of the book and supported
this and earlier efforts to communicate about plants in the Quran.

Like all teachers, I have learned much from my students. I wish to
thank them all. I want to make special note of Mohammad S. Al Zein's
helpful textual criticism, especially with *talh*. Sarah K. Boltz assisted

with images and the manuscript. Jay F. Bolin and David Cutherell did extensive editing. Students in my course on Plants of the Bible at Old Dominion University have seen, smelled, tasted, and felt Bible plants and their products with me over many years. I am moved by all their enthusiasm for plants of the Bible and the Quran.

Old Dominion University has provided me with a nurturing atmosphere for basic research for more than three decades. I am so grateful to be associated with an institution that encourages all types of research, even on plants of the Bible. The generous support of the Mary Payne Hogan endowment has enabled me to complete this work sooner than I expected, although it still has taken me 20 years!

It is impossible for me to acknowledge everyone who helped me in my research, but the list should certainly include Mohamed Aggour, Khalid Al Arid, Barakat Abu Irmaileh, Hani Abu Sbeih (deceased), Magzoub Omar Bashir, Faiz Bebawi, Mustapha Bouhamidi, Mwaffak Chickhali, Chris Dawson, Stuart Frazer, Atef Haddad, Eleanor Irwin, Jad Iszhak, Daniel Joel, Kamal Mohamed, Berj Mora, Abdel Baset al-Mouslem, John Musselman, Shawky Nasser, Fasil Reda, Sabir Barsoum Safa (deceased), Rob Sampson, Mats Thulin, Juliet Wurr, and Fatien Yacoub. Omission of any person who has assisted me may be understandable because of the over three decades and dozens of countries involved, but is still cause for regret.

While blessed by the teaching and assistance of many, I alone am responsible for any errors and misunderstandings in this text.

During the long gestation period of this work, I have been counseled, encouraged, and prayed for by a circle that includes Frank Batten Jr., Brian Campbell, Charles Holman (deceased), Henk Medema, and John W. Sizemore.

My four children (Jennifer, Rebecca, Sarah, and John) have patiently (usually) trudged over rocky ridges in pursuit of plants, bargained in Oriental bazaars, and overall been all that loving children could be.

I wish to express ineffable gratitude to my favorite Bible teacher and gardening instructor, Libby, my companion, support, and love for more than 40 years.

Introduction

PLANTS SHAPE CULTURES. This fact is evident by our ready association of certain foods with different cultures. Put another way, all cultures are influenced by the plants and the ecology of their settings. Original hearers or readers of the Bible and the Quran understood the symbolism implicit in the words, including plants and plant products in both their literal and symbolic usages.

In this book, I have included every plant mentioned in the Bible and the Quran, more than 100 plants, with one chapter for each plant with a true botanical counterpart. When there is disagreement over the identity of a plant or plant product, I have suggested some options, which, while informative, should not be taken as exhaustive. For each plant, I provide a short botanical description, including characteristics, habitat, and distribution, and I discuss the use of the plant, especially with regard to its scriptural context as well as uses today. I have also provided photographs that will help the reader to understand what the plant and its products look like. Most of these photos I took myself in the Middle East as well as in Western locations.

Many of the plants in both holy books have symbolic meanings linked to the scriptural imagery that is often expanded in practice. For example, olive oil is associated with spiritual power and sanctification, and it is used with that meaning to the present day. I have usually limited my discussion on imagery to texts in the Bible and the Quran, being fully cognizant of the vast corpus of literature on many of the

Ripening grapes in
July in the village of
Anjara, Jordan.

plants. I also offer thoughts from some basic literature and an eclectic mix of ideas I find of particular interest.

I have used a minimum of technical terms in the writing, and emphasized instead the features of the plants in plain language. The person interested in trees in the Quran, for example, need not know technical terms for leaf shapes. Rather, knowing that the *sidr* tree is viciously armed in nature will help in understanding the significance of an unarmed *sidr* tree in Paradise. Likewise, the priest studying the story of Zacchaeus will be assisted by understanding that the sycamore was the largest tree this diminutive man could find to climb up in so he could see Jesus.

The Bible places great emphasis on food. One of the major ministries of Jesus, along with teaching, healing, and casting out demons, was providing food. Libraries of books have been generated on the major plants and plant products mentioned in the Quran and the Bible, like grains, lentils, olives, and date palms, and these books have been written in diverse languages over millennia. These ancient plants are so important that at this moment, thousands of people are cultivating, harvesting, and processing these ancient staples on which their existence depends. I have discussed such significant plants at more length than others that play a minor role in the holy books, like onion and henna. Then there are other plants that receive very little attention in the holy writings but have recently been subjects of intense research, especially plants with medicinal applications, including ginger, black cumin, mandrake, and such well-known garden plants as garlic and dill.

Many examples of plants and their products embedded in Middle East cultures and expressed in the holy scriptures could be listed. Bread, just one example, is a clearly understandable image in the Bible. We know from archaeological data as well as from references in contemporary literature that wheat and barley were the grains regularly used to make bread in ancient times.

Trees are so prominent in the Bible that the main biblical messages can be summed up by four trees (Musselman 2003a): the tree of life and the tree of the knowledge of good and evil in Genesis (2:9); the tree that Jesus died on; and the tree of life in the last book of the Bible (Revelation 22:2, 14). In the Quran, trees are most frequently cited as gifts of a beneficent Creator, with the notable exception of the tree of Hell, *zaqqum*. In both holy books, fruits from trees are highly valued.

The Bible contains more references to trees and wood (over 525) than to any other type of living organism except humans. Of the 25 trees of the Bible, the date palm, fig, olive, pomegranate, and tamarisk are also included in the Quran. In the Quran, date palm is clearly described and mentioned more than any other tree (or any other plant, for that matter). This tree is still a dominant aspect of the landscape of the Arabian Peninsula. So it is not a stretch of the imagination to consider the date palm of the Quran as the same tree one sees in Arabia today. Unique to the Quran are the *talh*, the *sidr*, and the mysterious and foul "tree of Hell," or *zaqqum*: "Is this not a better welcome than the *zaqqum* tree? We have made this tree a scourge for the unjust. It grows in the nethermost part of Hell, bearing fruit like devils' heads: on it they shall feed, and with it they shall cram their bellies, together with draughts of scalding water. Then to Hell shall they return" (Sura 37:62–68, Dawood).

Other plants are less familiar to us today, either because they are not as widely used as they were in the respective scriptures; they were from a region outside the origin of the holy books, perhaps imported from afar; or the particular plant just cannot be pinned down accurately. These plants are translated in a variety of ways. The result is that the number of plants included in current translations of the holy books is probably higher than in the original texts.

To put names on the plants mentioned in the Bible and the Quran, botanists lean on two areas of study—ethnology (which I emphasize in this book) and historical use. Details of historical use can be found in such diverse sources as literature, philology, and archaeology. We are fortunate in having a vast corpus of writing from the Assyrians, Babylonians, Greeks, and Romans that details the usage of most of

the plants we find in the divine missives. In many cases, these sources present parallel details for both holy books. For the New Testament era, the classical writings of Pliny, Theophrastus, and Dioscorides are invaluable. Quranic plants, as well as those mentioned in the Hadith, have been widely explicated by such classic Arab writers as Ibn Sina. Philology of Bible terms is well documented, and I have referred the reader to several of these studies in the scientific literature.

The number of plants mentioned in the Quran (no more than 20 are explicitly cited) is much fewer than in the Bible (about 80). This fact is not surprising, considering the shorter length of the Quran and its link with a desert region. There are few plants that are obscure (except those that are supernatural).

How to present the plant words in English is a challenge, since in the case of the non-Western languages of Arabic, Aramaic, and Hebrew, they use a different alphabet, and Greek does not use the Latin alphabet. Further, philology is not limited to these languages in the narrowest sense, because the languages of the holy books also borrow from languages of surrounding cultures (see the "Aloeswood" chapter, for example). I have simply used standard transliteration into English without a formal system of diacritical marks.

No region in the world has received more archaeological attention than the Middle East. The recent publicity over the publication of the Dead Sea Scrolls shows the level of general interest in the region. The number of articles and books on Middle East archaeology is vast. Early contributions to the literature were largely descriptive; studies have become more analytical in recent years. With increased sophistication in analytical methods, it is possible to establish plant species and their products with a precision previously unimaginable. A good example is the work by Delwin Samuel on beer making in Egypt. She used scan-

Roasted green wheat is mentioned several times in the Bible and is known in Arabic as *frikeh*. This Palestinian farmer near Hebron has selected some suitable durum wheat from his field to prepare this delicacy.

ning electron microscopy to find that barley had been fermented. Likewise, workers can now use nuclear magnetic resonance and chromatography to make accurate analyses of ancient deposits like embalming compounds used in Egypt. The magisterial volume edited by P. Nicholson and I. Shaw, *Ancient Egyptian Materials and Technology*, is a treasure trove of information on an extraordinary diversity of plants and plant products, almost all of which were also used in other parts of the Middle East. I have drawn heavily on this work, in addition to the literature and my own research on traditional uses.

Traditional uses of plants may have origins in the Quran and the Bible or the sayings attributed to teachers in these books. For example, the Prophet Mohammed suggested that the leaves of *sidr* are useful for washing bodies before burial, and this practice is still observed in parts of Lebanon and no doubt elsewhere. Use of leaves ("fronds") of the date palm for the celebration of Palm Sunday is practiced by Christians not only in the Middle East but in other parts of the world. In a similar vein, wine and its significance are based on definite Bible verses. It is the less obvious uses of plants, however, that have particularly fascinated me—uses that are often poorly documented.

I know of no controversy in the translation of grapes in either of the holy books. But it is through learning alternate uses of grapes by local people that it is possible to shed light on some passages of scripture. One example is the practice in the Levant of harvesting hard, unripe grapes and powdering them to use as a flavoring for food. While this use is not explicitly noted in either book, the fact that unripe grapes are intensely sour lives on in English in the phrases "sour grapes" and "teeth on edge," both expressions finding their origins in the Bible.

Other traditions involving plants probably have their origins in pre-Christian and pre-Islamic cultures. One is the attachment of cloths and strips of cloth tied to trees, which are considered holy or mark a holy spot. Do these practices have the same root as the likening of men to trees in both the Bible and the Quran?

Even considering the biblical mandate of the Old Testament establishing the borders of the land of Israel to the River (the Euphrates), almost all work on Bible plants has centered geographically on Israel more or less within its modern boundaries. The work presented here, on the other hand, focuses on the region from southern Turkey to central Sudan, and from Cyprus to the border of Iraq, thereby encompassing most of the biblical neighbors of Israel. Likewise, there has been a tendency for writings on the plants of the Quran to be desert centered, when, in fact, the stories common to the two books took place in the same regions. An appreciation of desert ecology naturally is needed when writing about the development of Islam in the desert region of the Arabian Peninsula, especially the Hejaz region of what is now the Kingdom of Saudi Arabia.

We know that geology and ecology determine the plants found in these lands. This is true, naturally, everywhere on Earth. But the Middle East is especially diverse. In describing this unique setting, I can do no better than quote from the eminent George Edward Post (1838–1909), a pioneer botanist of the region, who in 1896 wrote the first English flora of that part of the world: "The region covered by this Work [his flora] is unequalled by any of the same size on the globe, not only for the thrilling and important events of human history of which it has been the theatre, but for its unique geological structure, its great diversity of surface and climate, and its remarkable fauna and flora. It is the meeting point of three continents, since Asia Minor must be regarded, from the standpoint of its Natural History, as belonging to Europe rather than Asia, and as such, a link of connection between them all. It is marked geographically by two mountain systems parallel to one-another, and to the coast, and extending from the Taurus to the latitude of Ras Muhammad [the southern tip of the Sinai peninsula]."

Post's words about the "meeting point of three continents" were prescient. Research based on the theory of Continental Drift, unknown to him, has shown that this region is where several major tectonic

Old date palms in the city of Jericho, known in the Bible as the "city of palm trees" (for example, II Chronicles 28:15), near the Spring of Elisha (II Kings 2:18–22).

Quercus calliprinos decorated with cloths honoring a Druze holy person, in May. Near Suweida, Syria.

plates come together, bringing the respective floras of Europe, Asia, and Africa with them. There is strong evidence that the diversity of flora in this limited area is due in no small part to the conjoining of three different floras.

Botanists are in general agreement with the system developed by M. Zohary and published in 1973 outlining three major vegetation domains in the Middle East. The first is the Mediterranean, which extends from Turkey as far south as the southern border of Israel and inland no more than 200 kilometers, except where modified by mountains. Plants in this flora, like olive and grape, are widespread around the Mediterranean. Much of the natural vegetation has been heavily modified by grazing; this largely treeless (or with stunted trees), scrubby vegetation is known as batha (a Mediterranean dwarf shrub formation; a slightly taller formation is known as garique) or maquis (a Mediterranean formation of evergreen low trees and tall shrubs with mostly hard leaves). To the east is the Irano-Turranian flora, which characterizes much of Iran and Iraq as well as parts of the Arabian Peninsula. This flora is adapted to much lower rainfall than those of the Mediterranean region. Many plants here are halophytes, often succulent plants, adapted to dry, saline soil. And a third domain is made up of plants typical of the Sahel that penetrates the Middle East via the Great Rift Valley. Species of acacia are representative of this flora.

If we look at the eastern edge of the Mediterranean on a current map of western Asia, Beirut is approximately at the midpoint. From Beirut, it is about 260 kilometers (200 miles) north to Adana, Turkey, and about the same distance south to Al 'Arish, Egypt, on the southern shore of the Mediterranean. A transect from Beirut to Baghdad gives the range of topography of the region. Beirut is built on the slopes of Mount Lebanon with very little arable land nearby, though the coastal plain widens both north and south of the city. Proceeding eastward, we cross the Lebanon ridge, which reaches its highest point at Qurnat as Sawda', 3088 meters (10,131 feet), the highest point in

Acacia raddiana, Wadi Feinan, southern Jordan. This area was an ancient copper mining site. No doubt acacia, which makes excellent charcoal, was used to stoke the smelters.

Barley in May, near Tayasir, Palestinian Territories.

the Levant. Here rainfall can exceed 1200 millimeters (approximately 47 inches), supporting the once extensive stands of cedar of Lebanon and associated species. Snow can be heavy and often persists. Alpine plants found nowhere else in the Middle East thrive here. The vegetation at higher elevations is a mix of high-altitude plants, floral elements from farther north, and several endemic species.

Continuing east, when crossing the ridge we see the narrow Biqa, which is the Lebanese part of the vast Great Rift Valley that terminates in southern Turkey. The eastern slope of Lebanon is much drier but still supports (or did support) forests. Much is maquis and batha. The Biqa is in the rain shadow of Mount Lebanon but is watered by streams such as the Orontes and Litani Rivers that form from precipitation deposited on Mount Lebanon. Agriculture is well developed in many parts of the Biqa, with broad plantings of grains and vegetables as well as vineyards. After crossing the Biqa, we climb the Anti-Lebanon Range. The flora of the Anti-Lebanon reflects a lower rainfall (200–400 millimeters, 8–16 inches), with drought-resistant trees, shrubs, and grasses. Agriculture is limited here unless water is available from wells and springs. Barley is about the only grain that can be depended on to give a reliable yield, though some fruit trees can survive. The Anti-Lebanon is a lower ridge, with its highest point being Mount Hermon, elevation 2814 meters (9232 feet). The common name of this peak in Arabic is Jebel al Sheik, or Mountain of the Sheik, referring to the snow that can persist on the summit into the hottest summer months, giving the appearance of a straggly, white beard.

The eastern slopes of the Anti-Lebanon Mountains are even drier, and aridity increases as we travel across the Euphrates River into Mesopotamia, east toward Baghdad, with an average of 400 millimeters (16 inches) of rain in the vicinity of Baghdad. The difference in the geology of the landscape is reflected in the buildings. On Mount Lebanon and in the Anti-Lebanon, buildings are made from stone, usually locally quarried limestone, while in rural Mesopotamia the traditional houses are made from mud or sun-dried bricks. Sustainable agriculture is only possible here with irrigation, readily available and utilized from the Euphrates and Tigris Rivers. In May this region is a verdant green of wheat fields, but within a few months it is scorched and intolerably hot and dry.

While this transect is simplistic, it illustrates the general pattern of rainfall and mountain ranges. There is tremendous local modification within such a large area that is diverse in geology. For example, there are several regions of extinct volcanoes. One of the most prominent is the area about 100 kilometers (75 miles) southeast of Damascus known as Jebel al Arab and the associated plain, the Plain of Hauran. In the Bible, the region is known as Bashan. While the soils here are derived from volcanic basalt and are fertile, the landscape is littered with large boulders, making mechanized agriculture difficult. There are other extinct volcanoes in this region, in parts of Israel and the Arabian Peninsula.

Farther south, along the Israel coast, the coastal plain is broader. The Plain of Sharon is a fertile region no more than 20 kilometers (15 miles) wide, which gives way to a ridge, then to the Great Rift Valley, then a ridge on the eastern side, then on, similar to the transect just discussed. Again, there is a system of two parallel ranges. The most remarkable feature is the Dead Sea, located in the lowest spot on Earth, 408 meters (1339 feet) below sea level. In this region, numerous elements grow that are part of the flora from farther south, known as the Sudanian flora. Within a few kilometers, it is possible to experience the Mediterranean flora, the steppe flora of farther east (what Zohary refers to as the Irano-Turranian steppe and desert vegetation), and, in the lower end of the Great Rift Valley, the African elements of the Sudanian vegetation.

At the latitude of Jeddah (about 21°30′), port for the holy cites of Mecca and Medina, the coast is dissected by a series of valleys that drain the arid upland into small, fertile valleys that can support agriculture. Beyond these valleys lies the formidable Rub' al Khali, or Empty Quarter, where no agriculture is possible.

To the west of Jeddah, across the Red Sea, lies Egypt, a vast desert with a narrow ribbon of green watered by the Nile River. Agriculture is fairly uniform in the Nile Valley, being most extensively developed in the Nile River Delta in the region of Alexandria.

I have painted the features of this region with a broad stroke. For the interested reader, there is a wealth of informative literature on the region. I would suggest beginning with the book by Michael Zohary, *Geobotanical Foundations of the Middle East* (1973). This work, on the plant communities, ecology, and plant geography of the Middle East, is a classic of botanical literature. The book is a rich compendium of information on climate, geology, and geography, and their relationship to the flora of the region. Zohary's work has informed this text in many ways.

Throughout the text, I provide scripture extracts that name plants, and I have followed these quoted pieces with the related Bible and Quran sources in parentheses. Following the book and verse citations, I provide the translation for that particular interpretation in abbreviated form; if all translations agree, I have not identified a particular source. The translations I have used and their abbreviations are listed here.

BIBLE TRANSLATIONS

ASV, Authorized Standard Version

JND, Authorized Version of John Nelson Darby

KJV, King James Version (more formally referred to as the Authorized Version or AV)

MSG, The Message

NKJV, New King James Version

NLT, New Living Translation

RSV, Revised Standard Version

   (The preceding seven references are from Electronic Edition STEP Files. Omaha: QuickVerse.)

NASB, New American Standard Bible, Lockman Foundation, La Habra, California

BIBLE TRANSLATIONS, continued

NIV, New International Version. Electronic Edition. Zondervan, Grand Rapids.

NJB, New Jerusalem Bible, Doubleday, New York.

QURAN TRANSLATIONS

Ali, A., transl., 2001. *Al-Qur'an: A Contemporary Translation*. Princeton: University Press.

Dawood, N. J., transl., 1997. *The Koran with Parallel Arabic Text*. London: Penguin Books.

Ancient lands of the Bible and the Quran. From May (1984). Adapted by permission.

Acacia

In Sudan, writing boards are fashioned out of Acacia wood.

COUNTLESS NUMBERS OF PEOPLE consume a product of acacia trees every day without knowing it. Just review the ingredients in ice cream and many candies and you will likely find gum arabic. In addition to gum arabic, trees in the genus *Acacia* are sources of other foods and of medicine and timber.

Acacia includes more than 100 species of trees and shrubs found mainly in the arid and semiarid regions of Africa. There they are often keystone species, that is, species that have an impact on the local ecology disproportionate to their biomass. Perhaps five species of acacias grow in the Middle East and Sinai. These trees are conspicuous in the desert because of their often slanted, flat tops. Leaves are small, an adaptation that helps the plant conserve water. In times of water stress, the tree can drop its leaves. Flowers are white or yellow and borne in dense head-like clusters. Middle East acacias are armed with thorns and prickles. This feature is reflected in the Hebrew word for acacia, *shittim* (implying something sharp), apparently alluding to the thorns that are necessary armament to keep grazers away.

Because of the slow growth of the tree, the wood is hard and dense, therefore heavy. The heartwood of acacia is dark red-brown and attractive when polished. The heartwood's deep color is due to deposits of metabolic wastes that act as preservatives, rendering the wood unpalatable to insects and resistant to water and fungi. Because acacia

Acacia albida, also known as *Faidherbia albida*, along the Khan River in Namibia. This acacia is widespread in Africa.

Natural exudation of gum from *Acacia raddiana*, at Wadi Feinan, southern Jordan. Gum can also be collected after the trunk is incised. While other species of the genus, such as *Acacia senegal* (the source of gum arabic), are better known for their gum, the gum from *A. raddiana* has also been harvested.

Sharp, strong thorns of *Acacia raddiana*, at Wadi Feinan, southern Jordan.

wood is especially durable, it is used in Sudan and other places in Sahelian Africa as a writing board.

Acacia trees are a source of gum, including gum arabic, which
is derived from *Acacia senegal* of Sahelian Africa. Gum was used in
the compounding of the sacred incense (Exodus 30:34), but we do
not know the source of this gum or whether it was derived from an
acacia.

Homan (2002) has studied the structure of the tabernacle, the system of tents used by the Children of Israel in the wilderness that provided a portable worship center with poles and stakes that could be set
up almost anywhere. The only wood used in the tabernacle was acacia
wood, likely made from *Acacia nilotica* or *A. albida* because other species of acacia would not have large enough trunks. Based on present
distribution of acacias in the Sinai, *A. albida* (*Faidherbia alba*) was the
likely source of wood.

All structural features of the tabernacle—the ark of the covenant,
the Table of Shewbread and its poles, the brazen altar and its poles,
the incense altar and its poles, and all the poles for the hanging of the
curtains as well as the supports—were made of acacia. This wood is
mentioned only in connection with the tabernacle (Exodus 37 and 38)
and perhaps Noah's ark. Because of the weight of acacia wood, Homan
(2002) suggests that the structural components of the tabernacle were
not solid, but smaller pieces joined together. If solid wood were used,
the structure could collapse under its own weight, and transport of
the heavy pieces in the wilderness would have also been a problem.

A tree referred to as *talh* is mentioned once in the Quran as a reward
for the "people of the right hand," meaning the people of Heaven:
"Those on the right hand—happy shall be those on the right hand! They
shall recline on couches raised on high in the shade of thornless sidrs
and clusters of talh, amidst gushing waters and abundant fruits unforbidden never-ending" (Sura 56:27–33, Dawood). My sources identified *talh* as either banana or acacia. *Talh* has been identified as banana
in several reliable classical and modern interpretations of the Quran

as well as in some classical Arabic dictionaries (Khafagi et al. 2006). Although banana is not native to Arabia, it is likely that Arabs were familiar with bananas, since banana was first cultivated in the Mediterranean region ca. AD 650, about the time of the rise of Islam. Further evidence is from etymology. Banana is from *banan*, Arabic for finger. Bananas, being sweet compared to acacia fruits, also fit well in the context of Heaven. The adjective used to describe *talh* in the Quran literally means "neatly stacked or piled one above another," descriptive of individual bananas in a hand.

The adjectival use of the word *talh* in the Quran, however, describes *talh* trees rather than fruits. A critical reading of verses 27 through 33 of Sura 56 suggests that the two trees *sidr* and *talh* are mentioned as sources of shade rather than fruit. Acacia has flowers crowded in inflorescences and grows in habitats similar to *sidr*.

Talh has also been identified as acacia. Acacia is thought to be the tree of Bai'at Rizwan: "God was pleased with the believers when they swore allegiance to you under the tree, for He knew well what was in their hearts, and sent down tranquility on them, and rewarded them with an expeditious victory" (Sura 48:18, Ali). It grows in the deserts of Sudan, Libya, Jordan, and the Arabian Peninsula. Its common name in Yemeni Arabic is *talh*, and it has lent its name to many places in the Arab world (Karkur Talh in Libya, for example). Farooqi (2003) states unequivocally that *talh* is *Acacia seyal*. In present day Sudan, the colloquial name for *A. seyal* is *talh*.

Acacia wood was commonly used in ancient Egypt for a variety of applications (Gale et al., 2000) including boat building. I have seen *Acacia seyal* used to build boats in Khartoum, Sudan.

Almond

Flower, bud, and developing leaves of almond. Northern Israel.

BECAUSE ALMOND IS THE FIRST FRUIT tree to flower in the lands of the Bible and the Quran, it is a well-known symbol of resurrection. In fact, because it flowers as early as January, it is sometimes possible to see almond flowers on branches covered with snow. Almond, *Prunus dulcis*, is a medium-sized tree with narrow, light green leaves. Unlike the fig and olive, it does not live to a great age. The white or slightly pink, five-part flowers are up to 2 inches (5 centimeters) across and appear in the late winter before the leaves of the tree develop. They are bee pollinated even though the pollen contains bee toxins (Kevan and Ebert 2005). Because fruit production is dependent on bees, almond growers often keep beehives near their orchards to ensure that flowers are pollinated.

Within a month after flowering, the almond's distinctive hairy, green fruits begin to develop. These immature fruits have a pleasantly sour taste and are sold by street vendors as a popular snack in the Middle East. My children enjoyed them when attending a Palestinian grade school. In the middle of August, the leaves begin to fall and the mature nuts are harvested.

Almond is related to stone fruit trees such as peach, apricot, and cherry: the seed is enclosed in a bony covering derived from the fruit wall. But unlike those relatives, the fruit of the almond is unusual: the leathery outer covering splits at maturity, releasing the stone.

Almonds are mentioned six times in the Bible, only in the Old

Orchard of almonds
in bloom in March,
at the base of Mount
Tabor, Israel.

Green almonds are a
delicacy in the Middle
East. Almonds of two
different ages are visible
on a Damascus vendor's
cart, in March. Those on
the left are younger. They
are sold with a packet
of salt in which the sour,
green fruit is dipped.

Testament, and not in the Quran. The first Bible reference is in Genesis 43:11 (KJV), where Jacob orders his sons to take some of the "best products of the land" as a gift to Pharaoh when they travel to Egypt to request grain. The best-known reference is Aaron's rod that budded: "Moses spoke to the Israelites, and all their leaders gave him one branch each, twelve branches in all for their families; Aaron's branch was among them. Moses placed them before Yahweh in the Tent of the Testimony. On the following day Moses went to the Tent of the Testimony and there, already sprouting, was Aaron's branch, representing the House of Levi; buds had formed, flowers had bloomed and almonds had already ripened" (Numbers 17:8, NJB).

The most familiar component of the furniture of the biblical tabernacle is the lamp stand, or menorah. The almond motif was part of the divine design for the lamp stand in the tabernacle. Moses was instructed to make the bowls of the lamp stand in the shape of the almond flower. The exquisite symmetry of the flower may be why almond is the model for the menorah. Almond buds and fruits were also to be present: "The first branch must carry three cups shaped like almond blossoms, each with its calyx and petals; the second branch, too, must carry three cups shaped like almond blossoms, each with its calyx and bud, and similarly for all six branches springing from the lamp stand" (Exodus 25:33, NJB; 37:19–20, NJB).

The reference to almonds in Ecclesiastes 12:5 is difficult to interpret: "When going uphill is an ordeal and you are frightened at every step you take—yet the almond tree is in flower and the grasshopper is weighed down and the caper-bush loses its tang; while you are on the way to your everlasting home and the mourners are assembling in the street" (NJB). The word translated "in flower" can mean two apparently contradictory things (Seow 1999): the reference could be to masses of white flowers on the almond tree, which can be an allusion to the white hair of old age, or it could mean "to be despised."

Almonds remain one of the most popular nuts. Although eating almonds is not mentioned in the Bible or the Quran, the ancients surely appreciated their culinary value and health benefits.

Almug

THIS TREE AND ITS TIMBER REMAIN the most mysterious of all woods mentioned in the Bible. The word "almug" was used only in connection with Solomon's construction of the temple, discussed in II Chronicles 2:8 and 9:10–11 and in I Kings 10:11–12. Bible versions differ on the translation of the Hebrew word *almug-giym*, rendering it as sandalwood, juniper, or some variation of algum. Through transposition of letters, the Hebrew word can be either algum or almug, generally considered to be alterations of the same word.

The dark green, shiny leaves of boxwood are valued in formal gardens.

From the verse and its context, the almug tree could be native to Lebanon, since it is mentioned with the better-known Lebanese timbers, cedar and pine (more accurately, cypress, as *Cupressus sempervirens* is assumed to be the tree translated as "pine" in many verses). In I Kings 10:11, the ships of King Hiram (King of Tyre) brought gold and "great cargoes of almugwood and precious stones" (NIV). For this reason, some Bible students have thought that the almug tree was native to southern Arabia (Ophir). Greenfield and Mayrhofer (1967) note there is little textual basis for associating Ophir with almug wood. Furthermore, the fact that Hiram's ships brought gold along with almug wood does not necessarily imply that almug wood originated in Arabia, only that it was transported by Hiram's men, who brought other products as well.

One possibility for almug wood is boxwood, *Buxus longifolia*, because large boxwood was known from the Taurus Mountains in southeastern

Boxwood grown as
shrubs in the national
boxwood collection at
the National Arboretum
in Washington, D.C.

Turkey. Hepper (1993) considers the box tree of the Bible (perhaps also the tree mentioned in Isaiah 41:19 and 60:13) to be *B. longifolia*. While this species is unknown in Lebanon, it does occur in the mountains just north of Lebanon in Turkey. Boxwood was highly valued by Egyptians for furniture and musical instruments (Gale et al. 2000). The latter use is significant in I Kings 10:12, where harps and lyres are mentioned: "Of the almug timber the king made supports for the Temple of Yahweh and for the royal palace, and harps and lyres for the musicians; no more of this almug timber has since come or been seen to this day" (NJB). Could this wood from Lebanon be the wood used in King Solomon's carriage (Song of Solomon 3:9)?

Boxwood is one of the best-known evergreen ornamental shrubs in north temperate regions and is a favorite subject for topiary. Leaves are small, shiny, and dark green. Flowers are unisexual, inconspicuous, and result in unusual fruits that open to expose black, shiny seeds.

So is boxwood a good candidate for this almug? Various scholars offer *Juniperus* (United Bible Societies 1980), *Aquilaria* (Löw 1967), *Pterocarpus* (Zohary 1982), sandalwood (*Santalum album*), or *Pinus* (Greenfield and Mayrhofer 1967) as almug. Linguistically the original word is Akkadian, and several ancient documents indicate the term as a valuable timber from the vicinity of Lebanon (Greenfield and Mayrhofer 1967).

To date, no one has offered *Taxus baccata*, yew, as almug wood despite the fact that it grows in southern Turkey in the same area as boxwood (Dinsmore 1932) and is known from ancient Egyptian carvings of the Eighteenth Dynasty (Gale et al. 2000). Yew wood is hard, attractive, and well suited for working with tools (Musselman 1999).

Another possibility is that the almug tree is now extinct. In the Bible, I Kings 10:12 notes that exceptionally large quantities of the wood were imported. Was this the end of the almug tree? Post (1901) offers the extirpation of the tree as one explanation for the mystery.

Aloeswood

Chips of the incense-containing dark heartwood of aloeswood placed on the lighter sapwood. Material courtesy Robert E. Blanchette.

"A LOE" IN THE BIBLE SUFFERS FROM a serious case of mistaken identity. Many might think that the aloe plant, *Aloe vera* (Agavaceae), used in lotions, shampoos, and other common medicaments, is the aloe mentioned in the Bible. But "aloe" is a completely different plant. *Aloe vera* is a shrubby plant. The juice of *A. vera* has no distinctive fragrance (Miller 1969).

Aquilaria malaccensis, on the other hand, is a tree that is found in tropical lowland forests in Southeast Asia (Baruah et al. 1982, Pojanagaroon and Kaewrak 2005). The heartwood of the agarwood tree, also known as aloeswood in English, is the source of an expensive, highly valued fragrance. In fact, the tree is in such demand that programs for planting trees to avoid cutting older trees in the forest are being developed in several South Asian countries.

The oil is distilled from the heartwood of the tree. Unlike many other woody plants with aromatic compounds, agarwood cannot be tapped or the material collected by incisions in the bark; the tree trunk must be destroyed to prepare the incense (Langenheim 2003). The wood is sold either as chips or splinters or as the derived oil.

How did agarwood become "aloe"? Greppin (1988) suggests that because Bible translators were not acquainted with true aloeswood, they simply translated the Hebrew and Greek words as aloe, a linguistically related plant name. This is of special interest, since Dioscorides

Tree in Bhutan,
where aloeswood
trees are planted
for commerce
to avoid further
damage to native
populations. Courtesy
Robert E. Blanchette.

Leaves of aloeswood,
Bhutan. Courtesy
Robert E. Blanchette.

notes that the aloe used by the Greeks came from India and that its source was a tree, indicating that its source might have been *Aquilaria* (Greppin 1988, Schoff 1922). Avicenna (Ibn Sina) (Welborn 1932) recommended it as a medicine.

In the Old Testament, the Hebrew word for the aloeswood plant is *ahaloth*. The Hebrew word suggests "sticks of wood," which would correspond with the way aloeswood is sold today. It is translated in the KJV both as "aloes" (Psalm 45:8; Proverbs 7:17; Song of Solomon 4:14) and, most accurately as lign (tree) aloe in Numbers 24:6: "As the valleys are they spread forth, as gardens by the river's side, as the trees of lign aloes which the LORD hath planted, and as cedar trees beside the waters."

The Numbers reference is intriguing because it is part of Balaam's curse-turned-blessing on the Children of Israel, which took place in the Jordan Valley. Balaam was a native of Mesopotamia, his home not far from the ancient major city of Carchemish. Was his familiarity with this plant, its uses, and habit a result of the use of aloeswood in that region? Aloeswood was widely traded in ancient times (Miller 1969). Cedar of Lebanon, which did not grow in Mesopotamia, is mentioned in this verse, suggesting that both aloeswood and cedar were used as symbols for beauty.

The Greek word *aloay*, used only in John 19:39 (NJB), probably refers to the incense: "Nicodemus came as well—the same one who had first come to Jesus at night-time—and he brought a mixture of myrrh and aloes, weighing about a hundred pounds."

Despite repeated references in the literature (Baruah et al. 1982, Pojanagaron and Kaewrak 2005), I have found no evidence that aloeswood was used by the ancient Egyptians.

Apple

Apple blossoms of *Malus pumila*, growing near Mancelona, Michigan.

ASK ANYONE ABOUT THE GARDEN of Eden and the apple will usually come up. Yet it is not mentioned in the first book of the Bible. In fact, except for Joel 1:12 and Proverbs 25:11, the apple, *tappooakh* in Hebrew (cognate with modern Arabic *toophah*), is mentioned only in the Song of Solomon (2:3b, 5a, 7:8a, 8:5b).

Because the Hebrew word implies a fruit that is fragrant, it could be that *tappooakh* includes other fruits such as the apricot (*Prunus armeniaca*). Apricots can survive less rainfall and hotter temperatures than apples (Juniper and Mabberley 2006), and they are fragrant, evidence that the apple tree of the Bible could, in fact, be apricot. Could the verse "A word fitly spoken is like apples of gold in pictures of silver" (Proverbs 25:11, KJV) be an allusion to the apricot tree in fruit? The word for apple is *tappooakh* in this verse. Some cultivars of apricot have leaves with a silvery undersurface, lending credence to apricot being intended in this verse.

The apple, *Malus pumila* (formerly *Pyrus malus*), was introduced to the Middle East long ago (Zohary and Hopf 2000) and remains a popular fruit in the region. However, cultivation is limited to areas with adequate water and moderate temperatures.

How did the apple become transported in legend to the Garden of Eden? Foster (1899) traces the development of the apple in ancient

Apricot in flower
in March, at an
Assyrian village near
Tel Tamir, Syria.

Apricot tree laden
with fruit in June, near
Deir Attaya, Syria.

times and how apple became grafted in a literary sense to the Garden of Eden.

Somehow the idea of Eve offering Adam an apricot seems heterodox because of the enduring legend, without textual support, of the apple of temptation in the garden. However, the apricot—no mean fruit itself in terms of desirability—may be the "apple" of Eden.

Barley

Like other grains, barley is enclosed in bracts that will be the chaff after threshing.

TWO OF THE MOST IMPORTANT grain crops in the world—wheat and barley—evolved in the same region that gave rise to the holy scriptures of Islam, Judaism, and Christianity. These grains are still cultivated on a large scale in the Middle East. While wheat remains the basis of life in much of western Asia, barley is scarcely used today for human food in the region of its origin.

Grain, including barley, was an important food source in ancient times, as mentioned or implied in both books: "He laid the earth for His creatures, with all its fruits and blossom-bearing palm, chaff-covered grain and scented herbs. Which of your Lord's blessings would you deny?" (Sura 55:10–13, Dawood); and, "For the Lord your God is bringing you into a good land—a land with streams and pools of water, with springs flowing in the valleys and hills; a land with wheat and barley, vines and fig trees, pomegranates, olive oil and honey; a land where bread will not be scarce and you will lack nothing; a land where the rocks are iron and you can dig copper out of the hills" (Deuteronomy 8:7–9, NIV).

Barley's inclusion among the "six species of the land" in the Bible indicates its value as a major food crop in ancient times. Its significance is also demonstrated by its being mentioned 35 times in 19 books of the Old and New Testaments, yet it is the more humble grain, cited less than wheat, which is mentioned 46 times, not including references to bread. That barley was widespread and appreciated is evident in scriptural narrative; for example, the man from Baalsha-lishah brought barley bread and barley grain for Elisha (II Kings 4:42), but Elisha ordered that it be provided as food for the people.

Unlike the Bible, when the Quran mentions grains it does not state whether barley or wheat is intended. Although both wheat and barley could be grown in Arabia, barley can produce a crop with very little water, so it is likely that this grain was well known to the Prophet and others of his time.

Less complex than wheat, the origin of cultivated barley is straight-forward. It involves a simple modification of the spikelet, which pre-vents shattering, that is, fragmentation of the grain head at harvest (Zohary and Hopf 2000), because when grain shatters at harvest, much of the crop is lost on the ground. The shattering wild barley of the Levant, *Hordeum spontaneum*, is now considered to be conspecific with modern-day cultivated barley, *H. vulgare*. In Bible days, much bar-ley grown was hulled barley: the crop was harvested with the grains surrounded by the subtending bracts.

Barley is planted about December in the Middle East, the exact date depending on the rains. The grain can be planted on soil without plowing, and for this reason it can be put in tiny plots in areas inacces-sible to draft animals. Further, barley can be grown in areas too dry for wheat. So it is often seen in semiarid regions, such as the edge of the Wilderness of Judaea east of Bethlehem.

Barley matures as much as a month before the wheat, as noted in the Bible: "The flax and the barley were ruined, since the barley was in the ear, and the flax in bud, but the wheat and spelt were not destroyed, being late crops" (Exodus 9:31–32, NJB). In the Middle East, bar-ley is mature by the end of April or beginning of May. When ready for harvest, the fields are a brilliant white, contrasting with the green of the durum wheat. Jesus was evidently referring to barley in John 4:35 when he said, "Say not ye, 'There are yet four months, and then cometh harvest?' Behold, I say unto you, 'Lift up your eyes, and look on the fields; for they are white already to harvest'" (KJV). Among more recent translations, this allusion to barley fields is lost, and the fields are simply referred to as being ready for harvest. Jesus's original hearers, however, would have understood the allusion to barley when "white fields" were mentioned.

Both barley and wheat originated in the Fertile Crescent, that arc of remarkable agricultural abundance that extends up the Euphrates River Valley, arches through extreme southcentral Turkey, and on its west lobe reaches down from Syria, through Lebanon in the Great Rift Valley separating Israel and Jordan. Agriculturalists now realize that the best way to conserve the genetic resources of these crops is in situ, even though thousands of accessions of seeds are stored at national and international centers for breeding and crop improvement.

In Bible times, barley was the main food of the poor and was also used for fodder (I Kings 4:28). It was valued less than wheat: "Yahweh says this, 'By this time tomorrow a measure of finest flour will sell for one shekel, and two measures of barley for one shekel, at the gate of Samaria'"(II Kings 7:1, NJB); and "Then I heard what sounded like a voice among the four living creatures, saying, 'A quart of wheat for a day's wages, and three quarts of barley for a day's wages, and do not damage the oil and the wine!'" (Revelation 6:6, NIV). Barley's lowly status was also reflected in other writings of the time (Watkins 1978). For eating, the Bible talks about barley being ground and baked into round cakes: "Gideon got there just as a man was telling his comrade a dream; he was saying, 'This was the dream I had: a cake made of barley bread came rolling into the camp of Midian; it came to a tent, struck against it and turned it upside down'" (Judges 7:13, NJB).

As noted in the dream, the usual shape of barley bread was round. Barley has a low amount of gluten, about the same as emmer wheat, so barley bread does not rise much and is flat. About the time of the origin of Islam, rice became an increasingly important grain. Barley was

The white barley crop (on the right) contrasts sharply with the maturing but still green durum wheat (on the left). This barley is growing in May, in a field near Aleppo, Syria.

still widely grown, however, as a fodder crop. I have never eaten barley in any form with local people in the Middle East.

Barley is still an important crop in the vicinity of Bethlehem, however. Small plots of barley are harvested by hand today, just as described in the book of Ruth, which has many references to barley. Boaz, a Bethlehem native, was a successful farmer, and barley was one of his important crops. Following the biblical injunction, Boaz left some uncut grain in his fields for the poor (Ruth 2:2, in accordance with Leviticus 23:22). Today, workers cut the grain, then tie it in bundles to dry. When dry, the barley is taken by donkey to the threshing floors, where it is threshed using modern equipment. If the ancient barley was a hulled barley, it could have been threshed with a threshing sledge pulled by an animal (Deuteronomy 25:4).

There are sundry references to barley as an important grain throughout the Bible. In Leviticus 23:10, the Israelite is instructed, "bring to the priest a sheaf of the first grain you harvest," probably barley because it is the first grain to mature. In I Corinthians 15:23, the Apostle Paul applies this to Jesus's resurrection. The jealousy offering (Numbers 5:15) is the only offering that specifically required barley flour.

Perhaps the best-known picnic in history featured barley bread: "One of his disciples, Andrew Simon Peter's brother, said 'Here is a small boy with five barley loaves and two fish; but what is that among so many?'" (John 6:8–9, NJB). A young boy brought his lunch to Jesus, which consisted of five small barley loaves and two fish.

Like modern residents of western Asia, most people today are not frequent barley eaters. While the grain is less desirable for eating, the forage value of barley is much greater than that of wheat. Barley today is usually found in specialty stores in the form of pearled barley (barley with most of the fruit and seed coat removed, which shortens cooking time), and is used in making soups, salads, and side dishes. Now considered a health food by many, barley is no longer just a food of the poor.

Winnowing barley in November with wooden forks to remove chaff, near Adwa, Ethiopia. Many of the agricultural traditions of the ancient Near East survive in the highlands of Ethiopia, little changed over the millennia.

As in ancient times, the barley sheaves are cut with a sickle. In November, in northern Ethiopia.

Beans

Large-seeded and small-seeded broad beans.

WHILE THE BIBLE PLACES GREAT emphasis on food, remarkably little is said about vegetables and fruits in either the Bible or the Quran. This probably does not mean those foods were less important then than they are today, only that their description is not essential for the quranic or biblical narratives. Onion, garlic, melons, and lentils are mentioned in both holy books. This limited menu is puzzling since so many widely cultivated vegetables originated in the Middle East—foods that are now part of our daily diets (Zohary and Hopf 2000).

The best-known diet mentioned in the Bible is that of Daniel, who requested a vegetable and water regime (Daniel 1:12). How these vegetables were grown or harvested is not explained in either the Quran or the Bible though cultivation must have been extensive. The sole vegetable garden in the Bible belonged to the evil King Ahab on property violently seized from Naboth the Jezreelite (I Kings 21:1–3). Ahab wanted to take Naboth's vineyard and convert it into a vegetable garden, which is puzzling since the Jezreel Valley is very fertile and many sites could serve as a garden. Certainly one of the crops that would have been grown in such a garden was beans.

There are many different kinds of beans and it is not certain which bean is meant in II Samuel 17:28 (NJB): "[They] brought bedding rugs, bowls and crockery; and wheat, barley, meal, roasted grain, beans, lentils"; and Ezekiel 4:9a (NJB): "Now take wheat, barley, beans, lentils, millet and spelt; put them all in the same pot and make them into bread for yourself." These references are the only two translating the Hebrew *pole* as bean (the Arabic *foul* is a cognate). However, based on archaeological data as well as current usage, it is likely that these are broad beans, *Vicia faba*, and chickpea, *Cicer arietinum*.

Broad beans are a staple in the Nile Valley of today, where they are a traditional breakfast food. They are also widely cultivated throughout the Middle East. Perhaps because the world now grows a number of different legumes—including peas, green beans, black-eyed peas, and soy beans—broad beans are not often sold in grocery stores except those specializing in Middle East or Mediterranean foods. Like other legumes, broad beans are highly nutritious and contain important proteins as well as fiber and carbohydrates. After soaking to soften the hard seed coat, broad beans are boiled and eaten plain, added to stews, or mashed into a kind of gruel. Some people are allergic to broad beans, a condition known as favism.

Sown in the late winter in western Asia, broad beans mature in the spring or early summer. The plants are large and bush-like, with white flowers that yield large pods with broad seeds. The seeds, when young, green, and tender, are relished in the spring and are prepared like butter beans or green peas. Mature beans are brown and flat in shape and, when dried, like other legumes can be stored for a long time. Two types of broad bean are grown in the Middle East: large seeded and small seeded. The small-seeded type is popular in the Mahgreb and India, while the large-seeded broad bean is favored in Egypt and Sudan as well as in the Levant. It was no doubt from a store of dried beans that David was supplied (II Samuel 17:27–28). The reference in Ezekiel, who was a captive in what is present-day Iraq, substantiates the widespread use of these beans in the ancient Middle East.

Chickpeas are best known to North Americans as the garbanzo beans of salad bars or, with increasing popularity, as the basic ingredient of humous. Chickpeas are an important part of the cropping

Flowering broad bean plants
near Senana, Ethiopia.

Developing broad beans in
May, near Kerak, Jordan.

Chickpea pods ready to harvest
in May, Tel Hadya, Syria.

system in many parts of the Middle East because the seeds can mature on residual soil moisture after the rains have stopped. In some areas, two crops of chickpeas can be grown in a single year. Plants are short with small, grey-green leaves and inconspicuous flowers. The legumes ("pods") contain only one or two seeds. In Syria and Jordan, green, immature chickpeas that have been held over a flame and slightly roasted are a treat sold along roadsides.

Both broad beans and chickpeas were important elements of diets in western Asia thousands of years ago. The few references in the sacred texts do not accurately reflect the extent of their use. Like several other foods in the holy writings, they were essential nutrition for millions of people.

Bitter Herbs

Chicory in a field near Bsherri, Lebanon.

A S WITH MANY BIBLE IMAGES, IT is not possible to say with certainty which plants are indicated by "bitter herbs." But the plant or plants represented by bitter herbs were important in Judaism, based on the following verse: "That same night they are to eat the meat roasted over the fire, along with bitter herbs, and bread made without yeast" (Exodus 12:8, NIV). From this verse, it is not clear whether bitter herbs were eaten raw (as tradition states) or cooked (not unlikely since both the meat and the bread were baked).

Many of the possible plants that would have provided these edible greens are bitter to the taste. Chicory (*Cichorium intybus*), native to the Middle East and common, has been suggested (Zohary 1982). This weedy plant is the source of commercial chicory (including radicchio), and because it is edible though bitter, it is a candidate for the bitter herbs associated with Passover. This species of chicory is widely spread in the United States, gracing railroad rights-of-way and other open areas with its beautiful sky-blue flowers.

But there are many other plants that fit the description, including members of the mustard family and relatives of chicory, including wild lettuce (*Lactuca* species) and dandelion (*Taraxacum officinale*), which are also suitable candidates.

Like other plants mentioned in a general way in the holy scriptures, care is needed when extracting meaning from a particular verse. In the case of this plant, clear identity is not essential for its cultic use.

Black Cumin

Black cumin seeds purchased in the herb market in Amman, Jordan.

"**D**OES HE NOT FINALLY PLANT his seeds—black cummin, cummin, wheat, barley, and emmer wheat—each in its proper way, and each in its proper place? The farmer knows just what to do, for God has given him understanding. A heavy sledge is never used to thresh black cummin; rather, it is beaten with a light stick. A threshing wheel is never rolled on cummin; instead, it is beaten lightly with a flail" (Isaiah 28:25–28, NLT).

The Hebrew word *qetsach*, used in this verse, which is translated "fitches" in the KJV, "caraway" in the NIV, and "dill" in the JND, is most accurately translated as black cumin in the NLT (the archaic spelling "cummin" is used in many translations). The word is found nowhere else in the Bible. There is little archaeological basis for translating "black cummin" as caraway (NIV). Caraway is not a Middle East plant, another indication of European translators' intercalation of plants known to them into the ancient texts. Dill is a possibility, though the description of the herb in the verse, implying a sharp, pointed beak, comports better with black cumin. The same word, *getsach*, is used for unrelated plants with similar architecture (pointed structures) in other scriptures (Ezekiel 4:9). In Old English, "fitch" may be related to vetch (species of the genus *Vicia*), a well-known legume fodder crop.

Black cumin is *Nigella sativa* and no relation to the well-known herb cumin, *Cuminum cyminum*. In the Middle East, black cumin is planted

Black cumin flowers with developing capsules evident in May, in a field near Aleppo, Syria.

Black cumin flowers. Several related species of this plant are grown as garden subjects, the most popular having the intriguing common name "love-in-a-mist."

in the winter and produces attractive flowers in the spring. This and related species are grown in the garden for their unusual flowers.

On Arab farms, I have observed farmers threshing the seeds of black cumin from the fruits by beating the dried plants with a stick in just the manner recorded in Isaiah 28. The jet-black seeds are pungent, with a distinct flavor. Black cumin is most frequently used to flavor bread, cakes, or other baked goods. The spice is either incorporated into the dough or sprinkled on top during or after baking.

Black cumin is one of the most widely used spices in the Middle East and has been for thousands of years. Black cumin seeds were found in the tomb of Tutankhamun (1333–1324 BC) (de Vartavan et al. 1997). Medicinal uses of the seeds have received much attention recently, especially for tumor suppression.

Like other spices in the Bible, black cumin is popular and is becoming increasingly available. The biblical narrative, however, deals more with the metaphor of the farmer taking different actions at different stages of the crop's development, all with an eye toward the harvest—a frequent image in the Bible. Pedagogically, this was no doubt clear to ancient hearers of the scripture, who would be familiar with the plants and the cultivating processes.

Bramble

Bramble, *Rubus sanctus*, near Nain, Israel.

MONG THE FIRST THINGS AN OBSERVER of nature would notice in the Middle East is the large number of armed plants with thorns, briers, and thistles. Plant armament is necessary to avoid being eaten by the ubiquitous sheep and goats that have roamed the countryside for eons. For this reason, the original audiences of the Quran and the Bible would have gotten the point—literally.

Jesus refers to this armed plant, bramble, in his teaching: "For every tree is known by its own fruit, for figs are not gathered from thorns, nor grapes vintaged from a bramble. The good man, out of the good treasure of his heart, brings forth good; and the wicked man out of the wicked, brings forth what is wicked: for out of the abundance of the heart his mouth speaks" (Luke 6:44–45, JND). No reference to bramble occurs in the Quran.

Scripture often does not distinguish among thorns, briers, and brambles, so although this verse differentiates thorns and brambles, we cannot be certain of the exact identity of any of the plants being referenced. Most likely the plant considered in this scriptural passage is the true bramble, a wild relative of the garden raspberry. Raspberries are in the genus *Rubus* of the rose family. This bramble, probably *R. sanctus*, occurs in abundance in the Middle East. Flowers are white or purple and fragrant. The arching stems are armed with sharp, strong prickles. The fruit is edible, succulent and sweet like other wild raspberries.

A curse on Edom, recorded in Isaiah 34:13, also refers to brambles: "Thorns will overrun her citadels, nettles and brambles her strongholds. She will become a haunt for jackals, a home for owls" (NIV).

Bramble, *Rubus sanctus*, in May, near Latakia, Syria. The bramble flowers in that region have a purple color. Fruits are valued by local people.

Broom

Broom survives in arid regions.

T**HE BROOM BUSH THAT THE** depressed Elijah sat under is common near Beersheba, the locale the prophet fled to after being threatened by the evil Queen Jezebel: "So Jezebel sent this message to Elijah: 'May the gods strike me and even kill me if by this time tomorrow I have not killed you just as you killed them'" (I Kings 19:2–4a, NLT). Elijah was afraid and fled for his life. He went to Beersheba, a town in Judah, and he left his servant there. Then he went on alone into the wilderness, traveling all day. He sat down under a solitary broom tree and prayed that he might die. "I have had enough, LORD," he said. "Take my life, for I am no better than my ancestors who have already died."

Called "juniper" in the KJV, the white broom, *Retama raetam*, is a member of the bean family and is unrelated to juniper, *Juniperus*, a genus of gymnosperms that is infrequent in the desert.

White broom is one of the most common plants in deserts and other arid regions of the Middle East. The many tall (up to 3 meters, 9 feet), slim stems arising from the woody base bear small leaves for only a short time during the rainy season. Attractive masses of white flowers are borne at the end of the winter. With no leaves on the plant, the flowers are especially conspicuous. The entire plant is toxic (el Bahri et al. 1999).

The underground portions of the shrub are an excellent source of charcoal that produces an exceptionally hot flame. This use is men-

Broom bushes in the dunes of the Wadi Arabah of Jordan. The shrubs have leaves in this picture, taken in December.

This broom shrub near Jericho is beginning to lose it leaves, a mechanism of water conservation during the hot, dry summer.

tioned in Psalm 120:3–4: "What will he do to you, and what more besides, O deceitful tongue? He will punish you with a warrior's sharp arrows, with burning coals of the broom tree" (NIV); and perhaps also referred to in Job 30:4: "They used to pick saltwort among the scrub, making their meals off roots of broom" (NJB). The Job passage is often translated as food from the broom tree, which is unlikely because of its toxicity. Rather, the meaning must lie in the use of the broom root as fuel. Because of its beauty and ability to survive under difficult conditions, *rotem*, as the white broom is called in Hebrew, is used as a girl's name in Israel.

Broom, like carob, is an example of a plant widely distributed in arid and semiarid areas but rare in holy writ.

Calamus

Fresh sections of the tough rhizome of calamus. Bruising or cutting the rhizome reveals an intense, sweet aroma.

THERE ARE FIVE REFERENCES IN the Bible to a fascinating plant translated as "sweet cane," "calamus," and "sweet myrtle" (Exodus 30:23; Song of Solomon 4:14; Isaiah 43:24; Jeremiah 6:20; and Ezekiel 27:19), the variety of names indicative of the confusion over which plant is intended. The Hebrew word is *qaneh*, a word used to describe other, unrelated plants with similar leaf shape.

The verses of the prophets Isaiah, Jeremiah, and Ezekiel clearly indicate the value of calamus and the fact that it was widely traded with nations in Asia: "You have not bought expensive reed for me or sated me with the fat of your sacrifices" (Isaiah 43:24a, NJB); "What do I care about incense from Sheba or sweet calamus from a distant land? Your burnt offerings are not acceptable; your sacrifices do not please me" (Jeremiah 6:20, NIV); and, "Danites and Greeks from Uzal bought your merchandise; they exchanged wrought iron, cassia and calamus for your wares" (Ezekiel 27:19, NIV).

Two plants have been suggested for calamus in Bible plant literature. The first is a widespread plant of the Old World, *Acorus calamus*. The second is lemon grass. Lemon grass is the common name applied to species of the genus *Cymbopogon*, most commonly *C. citratus*, which are grasses that produce a lemon flavor and scent. Many lemon flavorings in soft drinks are derived from this grass rather than from lemons. In central Sudan, villagers use native lemon grass to thatch huts

Acorus calamus, Hertford County, North Carolina. Calamus is the only Bible plant to have become invasive in North America. Its erect, narrow leaves may be the source of the Hebrew name *qaneh*, which is also applied to other plants with similar leaf shape.

The flowers of calamus are tiny and crowded on a thick, fleshy axis.

Ayurvedic herb shop in Matale, Sri Lanka, with bin of *Acorus calamus*. Calamus was widely traded in the ancient world and is a valued commodity today.

because the grass's aromatic content repels insects. But I do not think lemon grass is the calamus of the Bible.

Rather, calamus is almost certainly *Acorus calamus*. At one time considered a relative of the common houseplant philodendron, the genus is now known to be a distinct group of plants. It has an ancient history and was widely traded in ancient times (Miller 1969), evidence that it is the biblical calamus.

A plant of wet areas like margins of rivers and lakes, calamus is valued for the sweet fragrance of the rhizome from which various extracts are derived. The rhizome has been collected and candied, though the oil is recorded as being toxic (Leung and Foster 1996). In a review of its ethnobotany, Motley (1994) suggests that *Acorus calamus* is the calamus mentioned in Exodus: "Take the finest spices: 500 shekels of fresh myrrh, half as much (250 shekels) of fragrant cinnamon, 250 shekels of scented reed [*qaneh*]" (Exodus 30:22–23, NJB). *Acorus calamus* is not listed in a modern treatment of perfumery (Calkin and Jellinek 1992), but it is still used in medicine and cosmetics (Leung and Foster 1996).

Song of Solomon 4:14 indicates that "calamus" was grown as a garden plant. It is easy to grow and is a common component of home gardens in many parts of Asia because of its use in ayurvedic medicine.

Cane

PLANTS ASSOCIATED WITH WET-lands of biblical times are interesting yet few because of the limited wet-lands in western Asia. Some confusion exists over these plants' identity. Cane (*qaneh* in Hebrew) is an example.

Of the references to *qaneh* in four books of the Old Testament, the plant most frequently referred to is probably *Arundo donax*, or giant cane, which is ubiquitous where any fresh water is found in the Middle East. Especially prominent on hillsides, this plant marks a place where there is water even if

Calligraphy pens crafted from cane, in Damascus.

below the soil and not evident. Technically, cane is not an aquatic plant but rather a species that must grow near water.

Giant cane can be tall, up to 6 meters (18 feet). It often towers above other surrounding vegetation. Stems are unbranched, straight, and woody, like bamboo, therefore suitable for constructing huts, walls, and fences. Cane was also used as a measuring instrument, a kind of meterstick (or yardstick) in ancient times, such as the man with the measuring reed in his hand in Ezekiel 40 and 42. Apparently, the man holds a giant cane because of its durability and utility. And in Revelation 11:1: "Then I was given a measuring stick, and I was told, 'Go and measure the Temple of God and the altar, and count the number of worshipers'" (NLT), referring to a reed like a rod, implying something stiff, likely cane.

In Exodus 30, in the recipe for the anointing oil, the same word, *qaneh*, is used. Clearly a different plant is intended here, a fragrant

Cane is a true bamboo, or woody grass, which can be 5 meters (15 feet) tall. It can form dense, impenetrable stands like this one near Wadi Rajib, Jordan.

Flowering head of cane. Reproduction is mainly asexual in this grass plant.

Stems of cane comprising a wall, in Fuheis, Jordan. Similar walls for housing compounds are common in the Middle East.

cane. The use of the same word for unrelated plants may be because the word *qaneh* describes the shape of the plant.

In the New Testament, the Greek word *kalamos*, from which the Latin *calamus* is derived, is used for cane or reed in such passages as Matthew 27:48, where a sponge of vinegar was offered to Jesus on the cross: "And one of them quickly ran to get a sponge which he filled with vinegar and, putting it on a reed, gave it him to drink" (NJB). Another reference is Mark 15:19: "And they struck him on the head with a reed stick, spit on him, and dropped to their knees in mock worship" (NLT), where the reed was used for beating. In both cases, the plant that best fits the description is giant cane because of its length and strength.

Kalamos is translated "pen" in III John 13: "I have much to write to you, but I do not want to do so with pen and ink" (NIV). With a sharpened point, a piece of giant reed makes a writing instrument. I have purchased such pens made from cane in Damascus, where they are used for calligraphy. In some schools of Arab calligraphy, special emphasis is placed on pens made from giant cane, *Arundo donax*. Cane is also used to make simple flutes and for basketry.

Caper

CAPERS ARE INCREASINGLY IN demand these days because of the popularity of Mediterranean cuisine. Caper adds a piquant taste to sauces. Are the caper plant and its products mentioned in the Bible? While caper is common throughout the Mediterranean region, most Bible researchers consider it to be included in only one verse: "When the almond tree blossoms and the grasshopper drags himself along and desire no longer is stirred. Then man goes to his eternal home and mourners go about the streets" (Ecclesiastes 12:5b, NIV). Bible

Caper flower buds from Ramallah.

plant writers (for example, Zohary 1982) equate the word translated "desire" with caper, *Capparis spinosa*.

Caper is a shrub with sharp prickles and large, attractive flowers. It is striking, because it grows out of walls of old buildings. The plant loses its leaves during the rainy season and retains them during the dry season, which is unusual. The caper that is used for cuisine is the immature flower bud of the plant; it has a pleasant pungency and is pickled before use. I like the translation of the Ecclesiastes verse in NJB: rather than "and desire no longer is stirred," it is rendered "and the caper-bush loses its tang." Largest commercial producers of caper are Morocco, Spain, Turkey, and Italy (Sozzi 2001). The showy flowers produce a true berry as a fruit, which is sometimes pickled when young. The fruit has a shape somewhat resembling a human testis.

This fanciful resemblance to a human testis could explain why caper is in the NIV and other translations, no doubt based on the Doc-

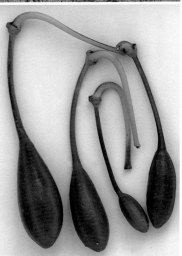

Caper plant growing from an old wall in Jerusalem. There is evidence from Uzbekistan that caper can actually destroy old buildings and monuments by growing in the cracks, expanding, and cracking the stone. Because caper seeds are bird dispersed, they often find lodging on walls and monuments.

Caper's large, showy flowers remain open for only one day and are mainly moth pollinated. In April, near Aleppo, Syria.

Fruits of caper.

trine of Signatures, a widespread belief that if a plant part looks like a body part, that body part will be affected by the plant. Simpson and Orgorzaly, in their widely used textbook (2000), attribute the Doctrine of Signatures to the Renaissance scholar Paracelcus, which I find unlikely since the doctrine is found in widely divergent cultures. Textual criticism provides little support for linking caper with desire (Todd 1886), and a recent review (Sozzi 2001) of the use of caper makes no mention of that plant's use as an aphrodisiac.

Whether the caper we associate with food is actually included in the Bible verse, the caper bush is indeed an integral part of the landscape throughout the Mediterranean region and the Middle East. Its spectacular presence on old walls and monuments quickly captures attention.

Carob

Carob pod and seeds.

L IKE ITS LEGUME RELATIVE ACACIA, carob (*Ceratonia siliqua*) is best known as the source of a food additive, locust bean gum, and as a substitute for chocolate. For these reasons, it is cultivated on a large scale in Mediterranean climates and is the basis of a multimillion-dollar industry. Quite a contrast to the way carob is presented in the Bible: food for pigs.

The carob tree is mentioned only once in the Bible, where fruits ("pods") are fodder for swine and become food for the Prodigal Son: "He longed to fill his stomach with the pods that the pigs were eating, but no one gave him anything" (Luke 15:16, NIV). The Greek word for carob is *keration*, from which the Latin name of the genus, *Ceratonia*, is derived. While "pods" could also apply to species of *Acacia*, the habitat of *Acacia* is too dry for swine culture.

A single reference to carob suggests that the tree might not have been well known on the biblical landscape. But carob is one of the most common and widespread trees in the Mediterranean region. A medium-sized, many-branched, evergreen tree, carob is a member of the legume family, which includes such familiar plants as peas, beans, and sweet pea. But unlike those legumes, the flowers of carob are very small, inconspicuous, and unisexual. The fruit is a pod-like structure about 15 centimeters (6 inches) long and contains about 10 hard seeds. The word "carat" is apparently derived from the Latin name of this

Mature fruits of carob near Ramallah, Palestinian Territories. At this stage, the carob fruits are harvested.

Unlike many trees in the Middle East, carob exhibits cauliflory, the production of flowers directly from the trunk of the tree. Botanical Garden, Stellenbosch University, South Africa.

tree, because the uniform size of the carob seeds was once used as a standard measure of weight, a carat, for material of great value. Today, the pods themselves have great value.

The walls of the pod and the partitions in the fruit contain high concentrations of sugar and proteins that are the commercial source of carob, often used as a substitute for cocoa. Locust bean gum, a common food additive, is derived from the endosperm of the seed. Local people in the Middle East boil the indehiscent (nonopening), hard fruits into a kind of dark syrup that is much like maple syrup. I find the taste delicious, sweet, and molasses-like.

In fact, instead of a chocolate substitute, this tree, which is common in the Middle East, was a food source for hogs in biblical times—hardly a commendation for a plant that is one of the better-known modern health foods.

Cattail

Cattail may be the aquatic plant in Job.

THE ARID MIDDLE EAST DOES NOT usually conjure up images of cattails, because they are commonly associated with wetlands. But at least one species of cattail is widespread in the region and may be mentioned in the Old Testament: "Under the lotus plant [*tse'el*] he lies, hidden among the reeds [*qaneh*]. The lotuses conceal him in their shadow; the poplars by the stream surround him" (Job 40:21–22, NIV). The King James Version translates the beginning of verse 21 as "under the shady [*tse'el*] trees ['*ets*]." This description of the behemoth includes its riverine habitat. It is unfortunate that NIV translators used "lotus plant" in this verse. Lotus is the common name applied to water lilies, most often *Nelumbo lutea*. But it is also the Latin name of a genus of legumes, *Lotus*, and species of this genus are not aquatic plants. Why is this mysterious plant linked with the likewise enigmatic behemoth?

Tse'el can mean many things, including "stalk" or "stick," in any case implying something slender. This could hardly be *Nelumbo*, which has large, round, usually floating leaves up to 1 meter (3 feet) across. A tall, slender, stick-like plant could be giant cane or common reed, both of which would fit here, except that *qaneh* is used later in the same verse. Papyrus could conceivably fit the description, except that in Job 8:11, the word *achuw* is translated "papyrus."

Could this mysterious plant be one of the other aquatic plants in the Middle East? In the context of Job 40, the plant should have the following features: forms a stand dense enough to hide the behemoth;

grows in a stream that might flood; be part of a guild that includes poplars, possibly *Populus alba*; and be a plant compatible with vegetation found along the Jordan River (alluded to in verse 23).

Of plants found under such conditions, the most likely is *Typha domingensis*, which is known in English as cattail. It forms dense stands and has long, narrow, vertical leaves that would be within the circumscription of the Hebrew word for something slender. The thick, heavy rhizomes can withstand flooding, and cattail is a common plant in the Jordan Valley, a region of high soil salinity, which this species can tolerate.

Whatever plant might be indicated in the Old Testament, the cattail is widespread in the eastern Mediterranean region and would be known to authors of the Bible texts.

These cattails are growing along the Zara River in the Jordan Valley.

Cedar of Lebanon

Female cones of the cedar of Lebanon. Chouf Cedar Preserve, Lebanon.

TREES ARE PROMINENT IN BOTH the Quran and the Bible. Arboreal references in these holy books reflect the place of trees in cultures of millennia ago: their uses, the local species of importance, and moreover their inspirational and symbolic significance, based on the perception of the tree as a symbol of life given by the Creator (Musselman 2003a).

People have always worshipped trees. Early tree worship in premonotheistic religions is recorded in numerous Greek and Sumerian classics. The ancient Greeks regarded trees as the first temples of the gods and sacred groves as their first places of worship (Baumann 1993). Groves of trees, often dark and mysterious, were thought of as haunts of spirits. The pagan use of trees and groves for worship is mentioned in the Bible: "places on the high mountains and on the hills and under every spreading tree where the nations . . . worship their gods" (Deuteronomy 12:2, NIV).

Both the Bible and the Quran refer to the utility of trees for food, animal feed, oil, fuel (including charcoal), and construction. In the Quran, at least two verses record fuelwood as a divine provision, a vital consideration in a desert culture: "Say: 'He who created you the first time. He has knowledge of every creation, who gave you fire from a green tree, with which you ignite the flame'" (Sura 36:79–80, Ali); and, "Observe the fire which you light. Is it you that creates wood, or

Lebanese geranium, *Geranium libanoticum*, carpets the floor of this preserved cedar grove on Mount Lebanon in May. Known as the Chouf Cedar Preserve, this stand of cedar is the largest and most intact of any in Lebanon; it is located at the extreme southern limit of the cedar's range.

Peony, *Paeonia mascula*, in May, in the Slenfeh Cedar Preserve near Slenfeh, Syria.

We? A reminder for man We made it, and for the traveler a comfort" (Sura 56:71–73, Dawood).

Trees are still venerated today in many countries of the world, including Iraq, Israel, Lebanon, and Syria. Among Druze and Muslim Arabs, certain individual trees are considered holy. These trees are often near the tombs of holy men or women, where visitors come to make requests. The pilgrims pledge to do good if the requests are fulfilled, and tie cloth, cloth strips, or rags on the trees as a solemn promise for their vows (Dafni 2003).

The largest and most majestic tree in the Middle East is the cedar of Lebanon (*Cedrus libani*). Not only is the tree impressive, perhaps one of the largest living things a person might see in a lifetime, but the tree's habitat is likewise spectacular—steep mountain fastnesses that, in spring, are carpeted with wildflowers such as *Geranium libanoticum*, *Rubia tinctorium*, and *Paeonia mascula*. Remote and green at high elevations on the Lebanon Range, both the tree and its environs have been venerated through the ages. Cedar groves are wondrously mysterious in the early spring when life-giving fog enshrouds the mountains.

Like its relative, the pine, two kinds of branching are found on cedar, known botanically as dimorphic branching, with short stems (shoots) and long stems (shoots). The leaves, or needles, are clustered in groups of varying number. Each group of needles is actually a modified stem, called a short shoot. The short shoots are borne on the long shoots, or branches.

Two types of cones are also produced, male and female. The male cone is a few inches (5 centimeters) long, worm-like, and falls from the tree after pollen is shed. The female cone is about the size of a lemon and is egg shaped. Like all true cedars (species in the genus *Cedrus*), the cone is erect when mature, not pendant like the cones of pines. Two years or even longer are required for cone maturation. At maturity, the scales of the cone break apart, releasing seeds.

Seeds are carried on the winged scales, which are like gliders, a feature that ensures wide distribution. Seeds are not viable for long and must germinate in cool temperatures. At these high elevations and low temperatures, growth is slow. Centuries must pass to produce the majestic trees that are now so rare.

An old cedar of Lebanon is noble in bearing. No wonder it is used in the Bible as an image of a mighty king—regal, strong, tenacious: "Son of man, speak unto Pharaoh, king of Egypt, and to his multitude; Whom art thou like in thy greatness? Behold, the Assyrian was a cedar in Lebanon with fair branches, and with a shadowing shroud, and of an high stature; and his top was among the thick boughs" (Ezekiel 31:2–3, KJV); and as a descriptor for the Amorites: "But as my people watched, I destroyed the Amorites, though they were as tall as cedars and as strong as oaks" (Amos 2:9a, NLT). Cedar is also likened to an upright man: "The righteous shall flourish like the palm tree: he shall grow like a cedar in Lebanon. Those that be planted in the house of the LORD shall flourish in the courts of our God" (Psalm 92:12–13, KJV).

Noble as a timber as well, cedar wood is resistant to decay, is fragrant, has a beautiful grain, and is easily worked. Apparently the tree could not be harvested without a royal decree. This was true for the building of Solomon's temple as well as the rebuilding of the temple in the days of Ezra.

The first construction use for cedar cited in the Bible was for kings' palaces (II Samuel 7:2). The most famous building of cedar, though not the largest, was the temple built by Solomon. In addition, Solomon built a magnificent house for himself entirely out of cedar (I Kings 7:1–2); so grand was this building that it took 13 years to complete, six more years than the temple. Earlier, his father had built a house out of cedar: "Look," David said, "I am living in a beautiful cedar palace, but the Ark of God is out there in a tent!" (II Samuel 7:2, NLT). The wealth of Solomon's reign, expressed in the hyperbole that runs throughout Semitic oral tradition, was indicated by cedar of Lebanon's being a common building material (I Kings 10:27). Other references associate the use of cedar with fleeting opulence. Like a Mercedes in the driveway, cedar was a status symbol during Solomon's reign.

The use of cedar in many different public buildings through the Middle East is well documented. For example, some of the beams in the roof of the al-Aqsa Mosque are cedar of Lebanon, mostly removed from other public buildings and therefore of great age (Lev-Yadun 1992).

A lesser-known use of cedar was in oblations for purification. One example is the cleansing for leprosy: "He will order the following to be brought for his purification: two live birds that are clean, some cedar wood, scarlet material and hyssop" (Leviticus 14:4, NJB). Details are not given, but it seems likely that small pieces of cedar were used for their fragrance. However, there is some confusion over whether this material or the oil derived from it came from cedar or from a species of juniper (*Juniperus*) (Meiggs 1982).

Timber, uprightness, purification, fragrance: to these aspects of cedar we must add a final quality, that of the most majestic plant. Solomon, the greatest botanist in the Bible, spoke about plants, suggesting that the cedar was the greatest: "He described plant life, from the cedar of Lebanon to the hyssop that grows out of walls" (I Kings 4:33a, NIV).

While the fame and planting of cedar of Lebanon has expanded around the globe, its natural habitat has shrunk. It is estimated that less than 3 percent of the original cedar of Lebanon forests are preserved on the mountain that gave the fabled gymnosperm its name. While most of the trees have been cut in Lebanon, there are still extensive forests of *Cedrus libani* in Turkey.

Perhaps because it is widely planted or maybe because it is such a definite, well-recognized symbol (Bikai 1991), the lore of cedar of Lebanon rapidly spread to the New World with European settlers. When these immigrants came to North America, in a day when Bible literacy was the norm, they called many different trees cedars, whether they were true cedars or even in the same family. For example, the widespread "red cedar" of eastern North America, *Juniperus virginiana*, is evergreen like cedar. And it does have a pleasant, enduring fragrance. But the cone has a fleshy, berry-like structure (known as juniper berry, one of the flavorings in gin), unlike the large spindle-shaped cone of cedar of Lebanon. And the tree is in a different family of gymnosperms. Nor is the name restricted to trees; many herbaceous plants have "cedar" as part of their name.

The transposing of plant names from the scriptures to local plants unknown in the countries where the books were written is not limited to the Bible. One well-documented example is the Mouride sect of Islam in Senegal. The founder had a vision under a giant *Sterculia setigera* tree. Adherents call it *touba* [*tuba*], the cosmic tree that, according to some Muslim traditions in West Africa, transcends heavenly and earthly spheres (Ross 1995). The Beja people of northeastern Sudan told me that *Euphorbia abyssinica* was *zaqqum* of the Quran, probably due to the caustic latex of the tree. I am sure that many other examples using both Bible and Quran plants could be cited.

Cinnamon

CINNAMON IN THE KITCHEN, BUT in the Bible? It is not the first plant or spice that comes to mind when thinking of the scriptures. Yet this well-known product of a tropical tree is a component of the holy anointing oil required for every priest: "Then the LORD said to Moses, 'Take the following fine spices: 500 shekels of liquid myrrh, half as much (that is, 250 shekels) of fragrant cinnamon, 250 shekels of fragrant cane, 500 shekels of cassia—all according to the sanctuary shekel—and a hin [archaic unit of measure equal to 1.5 gallons or 5.7 liters] of olive oil'" (Exodus 30:23–24, NIV). In addition to cinnamon, the related spice cassia (not to be confused with the legume with the same name) is included. Together, these two products of the genus *Cinnamomum* of the laurel family are cited seven times in the Bible.

Cinnamon quills inserted into one another.

The dried bark of *Cinnamomum verum* is the modern source of the spice cinnamon. While this tree can grow to be medium sized, it is grown in commercial plantations as a shrub. The stems are cut, the bark is burnished with a steel rod to loosen it, and strips of bark are cut off and dried. The curled, dried pieces are inserted into one another to create a "quill," which is the form in which cinnamon is sold. *Cinnamomum* is native to Sri Lanka, and that island nation is the world's largest producer. Oil can be distilled from the bark. An inferior but valued oil is obtained by distillation of the leaves.

Cinnamon, *Cinnamomum verum*, in the Royal Botanic Garden, Peridenya, Sri Lanka. In culture, cinnamon is pruned to maintain it as a shrub.

Removing cinnamon from the stems of *Cinnamomum verum*, at the Cinnamon Research Station, Sri Lanka.

In ancient times, cinnamon was almost certainly derived from *Cinnamomum aromaticum*, native to China but widely grown in east Asia and translated in some verses as "cassia." The Hebrew and Greek words for both cinnamon and cassia are borrowed words. It is therefore not clear in the scriptures which species was used, but based on records from ancient trade it was likely *C. cassia* (Miller 1969). Today, *C. aromaticum* is considered inferior, and most of the commercially produced cinnamon is *C. verum*.

Miller (1969) cautions us not to think of ancient uses of spices as entirely similar to modern uses. We think of spices as condiments, something to be added to food. For the ancients, these plant products were also ingredients in ointments, medicines, perfumes, embalming potions, love philtres, charms, and anodynes. And this is how cinnamon, as well as other spices, are used in the Bible.

Cinnamon as a love philtre is mentioned in conjunction with the alluring woman who says: "I have perfumed my bed with myrrh, aloes and cinnamon" (Proverbs 7:17, NIV) (O'Connell 1991). In Solomon's timeless love song, cinnamon is mentioned along with other plants, notably nard, saffron, and calamus (Song of Solomon 4:14).

In the Bible, cinnamon was used for its oil, although it is unclear whether that oil was from the bark or the leaves. Cinnamon was a highly valued commodity in the ancient world and is listed along with other luxury items in Ezekiel: "Danites and Greeks from Uzal bought your merchandise; they exchanged wrought iron, cassia and calamus for your wares" (Ezekiel 27:19, NIV). And the final mention of cinnamon in the Bible is on a similar list of luxury items in the last book: "Cargoes of cinnamon and spice, of incense, myrrh and frankincense, of wine and olive oil, of fine flour and wheat; cattle and sheep; horses and carriages; and bodies and souls of men" (Revelation 18:13, NIV).

Limited to a few occurrences, cinnamon is nevertheless found from the second book of the Bible to the last. It was highly valued and widely traded in ancient times.

Coriander

Fruits ("seeds")
of coriander.

MANNA AND SALSA? WHAT DO these two foods from different epochs and different cultures have in common? Coriander. Salsa contains the leaves of coriander while manna resembles coriander.

The Children of Israel were presented with a heavenly food, something they had never before seen. How would they describe it? By linking it to something they knew, in this case coriander: "The people of Israel called the bread manna. It was white like coriander seed and tasted like wafers made with honey" (Exodus 16:31, NIV); and, "The manna was like coriander seed and looked like resin" (Numbers 11:7, NIV).

Coriander is a widely grown annual crop in the Middle East and highly valued as a spice in Arab cooking. The seed (technically a fruit), when ground, is also used as a spice. More familiar to many are the leaves of the coriander plant, which are known as cilantro. There are several races of this widely cultivated crop used for the fruits (coriander) or for the leaves (cilantro). Cilantro is an ingredient of salsa and other Spanish and Mexican dishes. The two condiments, cilantro and coriander, are products of different subspecies of *Coriandrum sativum* (Diederichsen and Hammer 2003).

Though coriander is a familiar crop, it is not certain whether the word translated as coriander in connection with manna is the same plant because of the color ("white") and the appearance ("like resin"), which are at odds with at least the modern-day coriander.

Field of coriander in flower in May, in the village of Jdeidet, Syria, where coriander is an important cash crop.

Manna, the miraculous food provided in the desert, is included in both the Bible and Quran descriptions of the wanderings in the wilderness: "And [God] made the cloud spread shade over you, and sent for you manna and quails" (Sura 2:57, Ali).

The exact nature of manna is unknown. Perhaps the easiest explanation is that it was simply a divine provision, miraculously given. Or rather than being supernal, some Bible scholars have suggested that it may have been the exudate of a desert plant (Zohary 1982, Farooqi 2003). I have not seen these exudates, at least in desert plants. Looking like "resin" could support that view. More problematic is the relationship between the appearance of manna and the appearance of coriander seed. Coriander, at least the types now grown, has brown rather than white fruits.

Because it is linked with manna, the bread from Heaven, coriander is a well-known Bible plant and is grown on a significant scale in the Middle East today. As for many Bible plants, dogmatism as to which plant is actually implied from the text should be avoided.

Cotton

A SHRUB GROWN AS AN ANNUAL plant for its fiber and its seeds, cotton is mentioned in some translations of the Bible, but whether those translations are accurate is not clear. Cotton is the fiber that grows from the outer coat of the cottonseed produced by species of the genus *Gossypium*. It is native to both the Old and New Worlds, with at least one species in the Arabian Peninsula. With the advent of widespread irrigation, cotton is now grown on a large scale in Syria and has been grown for many years in Egypt. However, there is little evidence of its cultivation on a wide scale in Bible times.

Cotton fibers ready for harvest, near Maroua, Cameroon.

Whether cotton is in the Bible is debated. Most translations (for example KJV, NIV, and NJB) render the Hebrew word *boots* as linen: "He also made the Curtain of violet, scarlet, crimson and fine linen, working a design of winged creatures on it" (II Chronicles 3:14, NJB); and, "The garden had hangings of white and blue linen, fastened with cords of white linen and purple material to silver rings on marble pillars" (Esther 1:6a, NIV). The NLT translates linen in the Esther verse as cotton. It is more likely, however, that it is linen, derived from *Linum usitatissimum*, because cotton was not widely grown in the Middle East until the Christian era (for Egypt, see Vogelsang-Eastwood 2000).

Cotton is in the same family
as hollyhock and other
showy flowers. The hairs on
the cotton seed probably
aid in their distribution.

Crown of Thorns

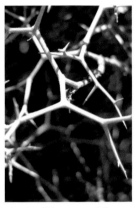

The flexible stems of the spiny burnet shrub.

THE BIBLICAL CROWN OF THORNS was probably made from the low-growing, ubiquitous shrub *Sarcopoterium spinosum*. This plant is abundant around Jerusalem and a conspicuous element of the degraded Mediterranean ecosystem in the mountains along the Great Rift Valley. Despite its Latin name, *Ziziphus spina-christi* (literally "spine of Christ") was probably not in the crown of thorns, even though it is often called that (this book treats it under "thornbush"). *Ziziphus spina-christi* is more frequent in drier sites and at lower elevations and grows to a much larger size.

Spiny burnet, the common name for *Sarcopoterium spinosum*, forms a mound-like growth among the rocks of the batha and garique vegetation in the Middle East. Leaves are deeply divided and fall during the dry season. True thorns are produced; these can be up to 10 centimeters (4 inches) long. Unisexual and inconspicuous flowers are produced in March. Small, fleshy fruits develop in May; they are edible but insipid, and to my knowledge they are not eaten.

Spiny burnet is a flexible plant; it would be easy to weave a crown from it. Obviously, the soldiers overseeing the crucifixion were eager to complete their task with as little exertion as possible, so they used a nearby plant: "The soldiers twisted together a crown of thorns and put it on his head" (John 19:2a, NIV). The flexibility is evident from a use that extends to the present time: farmers sometimes use the branches for cleaning animal stalls and other applications where a strong yet flexuous kind of broom is needed.

There is a widely grown houseplant called crown of thorns, but it is an introduction from South Africa (*Euphorbia milii*), and though well armed, it is not native to the Middle East.

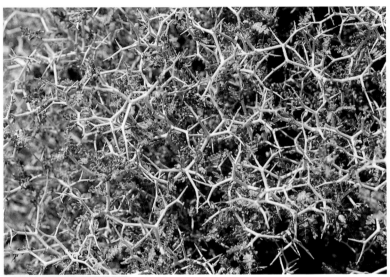

Leafy spiny burnet, *Sarcopoterium spinosum*, in March, near Jerash, Jordan.

Male (lower, yellow) and female (upper, red) flowers of spiny burnet, *Sarcopoterium spinosum*, in March, Dibbeen National Park, Jordan. Unlike some of its showy relatives in the rose family, these flowers are wind pollinated and therefore stripped of unnecessary ornament.

Cucumber

Snake cucumber at market near Nahr el Kalb, Lebanon.
Courtesy Houssam Shaiban

NEITHER THE QURAN NOR THE Bible explains the term "vegetable." Therefore, we are dependent on archaeological research that has shown what was eaten in western Asia at the time the Bible and the Quran were written. Interestingly, the most comprehensive list of vegetables—if it can be called that—is from the malcontent Children of Israel who, after leaving Egypt, desired the vegetables that they had left behind and complained to Moses. The incident is mentioned in both scriptures. In the Quran: "O Moses, we are tired of eating the same food, ask your Lord to give us fruits of the earth, herbs and cucumbers, grains and lentils and onions" (Sura 2:61, Ali). And in the Bible: "We remember the fish we ate in Egypt at no cost—also the cucumbers, melons, leeks, onions and garlic" (Numbers 11:5, NIV). Despite widespread cultivation of these vegetables in Bible times, this is the single mention of them, all well known then except for "cucumbers."

Because the common garden cucumber, *Cucumis sativus*, is generally thought to have originated in India and was not widely cultivated in the Middle East until the beginning of the Christian era (Zohary and Hopf 2000, Murray 2000), it is an unlikely Bible plant. Rather, the cucumber mentioned is actually a kind of melon, called chate melon, *Cucurbita pepo* var. *flexuosus*, also known as *Cucurbita pepo* subspecies *ovifera*, eaten as a cucumber. Its flavor is milder than that of the common garden cucumber and the flesh is firmer.

Snake cucumber with flowers and developing fruits, in July, Tel Hadya, Syria. Courtesy Atef Haddad.

Snake cucumbers arriving at market in Lebanon. Courtesy Houssam Shaiban.

Common in Sudan and Egypt, where it is known in Arabic as *ajjour*, this cucumber usually grows coiled, hence the English name "snake cucumber." When I lived in Sudan, *ajjour* was the only cucumber available in the market, with large specimens up to almost 1 meter (3 feet) long. In Lebanon, *Cucurbita pepo* var. *flexuosus* is also commonly grown and known as *mekteh*; there the young, small cucumbers are often pickled. Apparently, snake cucumber was grown at one time in Europe (Janick and Paris 2006).

The "vegetable verse" in Numbers 11 is often viewed as the produce section of the Bible, and to a large extent that is true. The "cucumber" in this verse, however, is not a cucumber but a relative of the cantaloupe.

Cumin

The "seeds" of cumin.

THE SPICE CUMIN, OR CUMMIN (archaic), derived from the ground "seeds" of the plant, is an essential component of east Asian as well as Mexican cuisine and for the same reason. Arab traders took the spice to India as well as to Spain. From Spain, it traveled to the New World.

In the Bible, cumin was used as a kind of contribution for worship: "Woe to you, teachers of the law and Pharisees, you hypocrites! You give a tenth of your spices—mint, dill and cummin. But you have neglected the more important matters of the law—justice, mercy and faithfulness. You should have practiced the latter, without neglecting the former" (Matthew 23:23, NIV).

Cumin, *Cuminum cyminum*, is also mentioned in the Old Testament, unlike dill, mint, or rue. There is a great deal of similarity among the words used for cumin in Hebrew, Greek, and Arabic, lending strong support to the identity of this popular herb in the holy books. Cumin has been used for thousands of years in Egypt and surrounding countries (Murray 2000).

A relative of dill, cumin is an easily grown annual plant. Like most herbs, cumin is planted in the winter and harvested in May in the Middle East. It is grown for its seeds. The fruits of cumin contain "seeds," each being technically a mericarp; the fruit splits rather than opening. Cumin seeds are usually ground into a spice that is used to flavor bread, pastries, and other dishes. Once ground, cumin soon loses

Cumin in flower in the Jordan River Valley, Jordan.

Cumin ready for harvest in northern Syria. Farmers in this part of Mesopotamia grow cumin as a cash crop because of the culinary demand for the spice.

its pungency. Cumin is mentioned three times in Isaiah 28 (Isaiah 28:25–28).

Cumin must have been well known to the target audiences of the Old Testament, as the Isaiah reference suggests, as well as to the hearers of Jesus. The New Testament reference indicates how highly valued cumin was as a spice.

Cypress

Cypress, *Cupressus sempervirens*, showing the distinctive fleshy cones of this genus.

T HE WOODS USED IN BUILDING Solomon's temple have long posed a difficulty for Bible students. The beloved King James Version refers to fir and the New International Version refers to pine, when describing the trees that Hiram, King of Tyre, contracted to send to Solomon for the edifice. Hiram notes that he will bring these timbers from Lebanon: "Your servants will bring these down from Lebanon to the sea, and I shall have them towed by sea to any place you name" (I Kings 5:9, NJB), strongly implying that the trees were found on that mountain range. Further evidence for the montane habitat of these trees is this passage: "The glory of Lebanon will come to you, the pine, the fir and the cypress together, to adorn the place of my sanctuary; and I will glorify the place of my feet" (Isaiah 60:13, NIV). What are these trees?

Relatively few trees are native to the Middle East. So it is confusing what the trees in these verses might be and how certain translators have come up with pine, fir, and cypress. (Translation of the tree cedar of Lebanon poses no problem.) The two most prevalent pines in the region are *Pinus halepensis,* Aleppo pine; and *P. brutia*, Calabrian pine. The only true fir that is found in the Levant is *Abies cilicica* (Cilician fir). The third tree that is referred to in several translations, from the Hebrew, *berosh*, is cypress, *Cupressus sempervirens*, often translated as

This plant is the fastigate (narrow) form of *Cupressus sempervirens* in the mountains near the Saladin Citadel in northern Syria, widely planted since Roman times. The female cones are evident; they can remain on the tree for many years and may be an adaptation to a fire-based ecology. The tree compensates for a lack of fire by producing some cones that can open without heat.

Juniper, *Juniperus oxycedrus*, on Mount Lebanon. Courtesy Houssam Shaiban.

pine or fir. To establish which trees are being discussed, we must consider both the linguistic and ecologic factors.

In terms of habitat, the pines and the cypress are not found at higher altitudes. The cilician fir is a component of cedar forests but is found only in the northern part of the Lebanon Range. It is possible that Hiram's men cut those trees and brought them south to Tyre. But unless the wood had considerable value in a specialty application, this seems unlikely. The remaining tree, cypress, is found extensively throughout the Middle East and is well represented in archaeological finds in Egypt (Gale et al. 2000).

Like the cedar of Lebanon, cypress is a conifer—a cone-bearing tree with hard, durable wood. Its leaves are different from pine and cedar: they are tiny and scale-like. The female cones are round and about the size of a walnut.

Most of the cypress trees I have seen in the Middle East are narrow in form (fastigate), with erect branches usually close to the ground. Because of this growth habit, its attractive green color, and its ease of culture, cypress is a popular tree for planting along roads, in parks, and at homesites. I have seen Byzantine mosaics in Medaba, Jordan, that included this tree form, indicating that this fastigate tree was known to the people of Bible times. Farjon (2005) points out, however, that the abundance of the fastigate form may be an artifact of widespread planting of that tree since Roman times and that natural forests of cypress generally had spreading crowns. Seeds from a single cypress might include both open-crown and fastigate forms.

Cypress wood, which is strong and durable, was highly valued by ancients, especially for monumental doors and statues (Meiggs 1982). Cypress was counted among valuable trees as evidenced in the Bible, where cypress (*berosh* in Hebrew) is linked with cedar and oak: "Open your doors, Lebanon, so that fire may devour your cedar forests. Weep, you cypress trees, for all the ruined cedars; the most majestic ones have fallen" (Zechariah 11:1–2a, NIV). Therefore, while it is not certain that cypress was used in Solomon's temple, it is a likely candidate, based on uses of cypress in other ancient monumental buildings. "Gopher wood" is mentioned in regard to Noah's ark: "Make thee an ark of gopher wood; rooms shalt thou make in the ark, and shalt pitch it within and without with pitch" (Genesis 6:14, KJV). Although gopher wood is a mystery, several authors have suggested that it is cypress (NIV).

Another group of trees is sometimes conflated with *berosh*, the junipers (genus *Juniperus*). Juniper is represented in the Levant by three or four species that can reach a size suitable for timber. *Juniperus oxycedrus* and *J. excelsa* grow at higher elevations (along with the less frequent *J. drupacea*), while *J. phoenicea* is common in drier regions. *Juniperus phoenicea* has been found in archaeological sites in southern Israel (Liphschitz et al. 1981).

Cypress, like cedar of Lebanon, has inspired numerous, though misapplied, common names for other plants. It was one of the most important and durable timber trees in the ancient eastern (Mediterranean) world.

Date Palm

A commercial planting of date palm in the Jordan Valley, Israel.

T HE DATE PALM IS THE MOST prominent tree, and often the only tree, of desert regions in the Middle East. While common, it is not pedestrian. Rather, the date palm is remarkably adapted to regions of little water and high soil salinity.

Phoenix dactylifera, date palm, is the most frequently cited plant in the Quran: "We send down blessed water from the sky with which We bring forth gardens and the harvest grain, and tall palm-trees laden with clusters of dates, a sustenance for men; thereby giving new life to a dead land. Such shall be the Resurrection" (Sura 50:9–11, Dawood). The tree is cited in 10 places in the Quran.

This native of the hot, arid regions of the desert, with its tall, solitary trunk and huge, spreading leaves, is a dominant feature of the Middle East landscape. There are numerous varieties of dates. Dates can be yellow or red. An Arab proverb says that there are as many different kinds of dates as days in the year.

In both holy books, palm trees are likened to humans. This noble

Grove of date palm trees in the ruins of the ancient Phoenician city of Byblos, modern day Jbeil, Lebanon. Sprouting from the base is evident; the sprouts can be used to start new trees.

tree is a picture of the upright: "The righteous shall flourish like a palm tree, he shall grow like a cedar of Lebanon" (Psalm 92:12, NIV); and, "This thy stature is like to a palm tree" (Song of Solomon 7:7, KJV).

In the Quran, judgment on evil men is likened to upturned date palms, an image the hearers would understand as an act of supernatural power: "Which snatched away men as though they were palm trees pulled out by the roots" (Sura 54:20, Ali). The date palm is a site of execution of the sorcerers in the court of Pharoah at the time of Moses.

Date palm is mentioned several times with regard to traditions in the life of the Prophet Mohammad. One incident illustrates this well, using the diversity among types of date palms. During one battle, it was not clear who the raiders were or where they came from. Mohammed examined the date palm pits in camel droppings and was able to establish the town of his enemies based on his knowledge of the types of dates that grow there.

In modern Hebrew and Arabic, the ancient biblical name of the fruit, *tamar*, is preserved. Tamar is a feminine name used both in Bible and modern times.

Phoenix dactylifera is native to the Middle East; most of its relatives grow in Africa (Zohary and Hopf 2000). Wild date palm trees are common in the Dead Sea region, where they can inhabit brackish water in areas where other plants will not grow.

In addition to its fruit, the date palm was once valued for its leaves, which were used to make baskets, roofs, and mats. Also, ancients used ropes in much the same way as in North America and Europe years ago: "Woe to those who drag guilt along by the reins of duplicity, drag along sin as though with a cart rope" (Isaiah 5:18, NJB). The Bible does not give us the source of this cordage, but palm leaves can be used for weaving rope. Leaves of a palm common in Egypt, *Hyphaene thebaica*, are still a source of cordage. In addition, the trunk of the date palm was used for building, though the wood is not suitable for furniture (Gale et al. 2000).

Yellow dates near the Baptismal Site, Jordan Valley, Jordan. Fresh dates are considered a delicacy in many Arab countries, though they often have an astringency not found in dried dates.

Wild date palms in a narrow wadi near the Dead Sea, Jordan.

Because date palms are unisexual, the female trees are planted with only an occasional male tree to insure fertilization of the flowers. The palm produces shoots from its base; these are removed to strengthen the main stem, but they can also be used to establish new plants. By planting these shoots, the grower knows the sex of the plant as well as the variety and is thus able to plant a grove of trees of known gender and provenance. If the trees were grown from seed, approximately half would be male and half female.

The date palm produces masses of small, white flowers on its large branches in the spring. At least one translation of the Quran refers to a drink in Paradise flavored with palm blossoms: "Surely the devotees will drink cups flavoured with palm blossoms from a spring of which the votaries of God will drink and make it flow in abundance" (Sura 76:5–6, Ali; in Dawood's translation, he refers to this as camphor-flavored water). Because the date palm is wind pollinated, the flowers have the most basic equipment and do not need showy appendages. In nature, the fruits' seeds are dispersed by bats. Mature dates are harvested in late summer and early autumn.

Ripe dates are rich in sugar, up to 60 percent, providing a valuable food source. Because of the high sugar content, they can be used for fermentation. At least one commentator on the Quran suggests that dates (as well as grapes) can be used for fermentation: "And the fruits of the palm and the vine, from which you derive intoxicants and wholesome food" (Sura 16:67, Dawood). Since wine is proscribed in the Quran, this verse might apply to the preparation of vinegar.

The palm was prominent in the decoration of Solomon's temple. In I Kings 6:29, 32, 35 and also II Chronicles 3:5, the walls of the temple were described as adorned with palm trees. The palm tree has an even greater role in the temple of Ezekiel (40:31), where the palm tree was inscribed on the posts of the chambers, the gate, and the posts of various gates.

Surely the best-known reference to the palm in the New Testament is the paving of the streets in Jesus's time for his passage: "The next day, the news that Jesus was on the way to Jerusalem swept through the city. A large crowd of Passover visitors took palm branches and went down the road to meet him" (John 12:12–13a). We can assume that these trees were common in ancient Jerusalem.

The date palm is the most distinctive of all trees discussed in the holy books, with its single, towering trunk topped by massive leaves that radiate from the crown. This alone would make the plant inspiring. But it also yields a delicious fruit high in sugar that is easily stored. All of this from a tree that can grow in the desert.

Dill

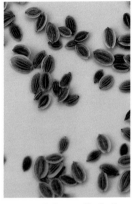

Dill "seeds," actually fruits.

WHEN I THINK OF DILL, I think of dill pickles. One of the best-known uses of this ancient herb in modern Western societies is for flavoring pickles.

Dill was also widely appreciated in ancient times, recorded from ancient Egypt and elsewhere. Dill was so valued that it was used as an offering: "Woe to you, teachers of the law and Pharisees, you hypocrites! You give a tenth of your spices—mint, dill and cummin. But you have neglected the more important matters of the law—justice, mercy and faithfulness. You should have practiced the latter, without neglecting the former" (Matthew 23:23, NIV).

Dill, *Anethum graveolens*, is mentioned in the Bible only in that one spot. While the herb is well known as a component of pickles, dill is widely grown throughout the world and is used to flavor many dishes and sauces. Both the seed and the leaves are used. Dill seed was found in the tombs of Egyptian kings, demonstrating its long use in the Middle East (Vartavan and Amorós 1997). Dill is thought to have evolved in the region (Zohary and Hopf 2000).

It is probably difficult for those of us living in the twenty-first century, with our ready access to herbs and spices from around world, to understand how valuable these condiments were in the ancient world for their power to add flavor and variety to foods—and that they would be so valuable, they were used for tithing.

Flowering dill, *Anethum graveolens*, **in May, near Brumanna, Lebanon.**
Courtesy Houssam Shaiban.

Ebony

Compound leaves of ebony, genus *Dalbergia*, in the Royal Botanic Garden, Peradenya, Sri Lanka.
Courtesy Kushan Tennakoon.

SEVERAL CITIES AND THEIR CIVILI-zations are mentioned in the Bible as examples of religious, political, and economic power. The best-known example is Babylon. Perhaps less known is Tyre, a port city located only a few miles north of the border of Israel in what is modern-day Lebanon.

Little remains of this original city of the industrious Phoenicians. But at one time, Tyre was one of the most prosperous cities in the world. Ezekiel 27 describes the commercial activity of Tyre, and enumerates the products, their sources, and the countries that trafficked in them. This chapter of the Bible offers an important comment on the commodities of the ancient world and how they were marketed. In particular, it mentions ebony, one of the most valuable items, and the reference is the only mention of ebony in the Bible: "The people of Dedan [Rhodes?] traded with you; many islands were your customers and paid you in ivory tusks and ebony" (Ezekiel 27:15, NJB).

The problem in interpretation is that several trees produce wood known in the ancient world as "ebony" (Dixon 1974, Meiggs 1982). Almost all of the ebony identified in Egyptian archaeology is from *Dalbergia melanoxylon*, a legume tree native to Africa that has hard, black heartwood. A similar wood is derived from *Diospyros ebenum*, native to southern India and a close relative of the common persimmon of eastern North America. (Many woods are sold as ebony today, but

True ebony, genus *Dalbergia*, in the Royal Botanic Garden, Peradenya, Sri Lanka.
Courtesy Kushan Tennakoon.

Another source of ebony, this one African in origin. There is evidence that wood from this tree, *Diospyros ebenum*, was widely traded in ancient times. Royal Botanic Garden, Peradenya, Sri Lanka.

these are from related trees or from different timbers with features like ebony).

Ebony is the jet-black heartwood obtained from older trees. Its color, dense grain, durability, and easy workability made it valuable for wood carvers, and it was a most desirable wood for furniture for the wealthy, especially when inlaid with ivory (Meiggs 1982, Gale et al. 2000). Just as the single verse links ivory and ebony, ivory, too, is easily worked, beautiful, and durable, and is often incorporated into ebony idols.

Ebony was an import into the Middle East and may have been derived from more than one kind of tree. Whatever tree it was, it is clear that the wood was highly valued.

Fig

Flowers of the fig near Um Qais, Jordan. At this stage, the wasp enters and pollinates the flowers.

FIG TREES HAVE BEEN VALUED FOR millennia for their sweet, delicious fruits. Figs are basic ingredients in several modern foods, including the cookies known as Fig Newton.

Because of their ubiquity and utility in the Middle East, figs have a prominent role in both the Quran and the Bible. In fact, one entire sura of the Quran is called simply "The Fig": "By the fig, and by the olive! By Mount Sinai, and by this inviolate city. We created man in a most noble image and in the end We shall reduce him to the lowest of the low: except the believers who do good works, for theirs shall be a boundless recompense. What then after this can make you deny the last judgement? Is God not the best of judges?" (Sura 95:1–8, Dawood). I have quoted the entire passage because of the association of fig with testimony and judgment, a theme also present in the Bible.

For example, Jeremiah told the people to submit to Nebuchednezzar, who had conquered their land. If they did, they would be blessed; if not, disaster would come upon them. To make this point, two baskets of figs are set in front of the temple to signify two groups of Jews— good figs and bad figs. Those who, in compliance with the word of the Lord to Jeremiah, had submitted to the King of Babylon are regarded as good and would be planted in the land: "The Lord showed me two baskets of figs placed in front of the temple of the Lord. One basket had very good figs, like those that ripen early; the other basket had very poor figs, so bad they could not be eaten. Then the Lord asked me, 'What do you see, Jeremiah?' 'Figs,' I answered. 'The good ones are very good, but the poor ones are so bad they cannot be eaten.'"

" 'But like the poor figs, which are so bad they cannot be eaten, says the LORD, 'so will I deal with Zedekiah, king of Judah, his officials and the survivors from Jerusalem, whether they remain in this land or live in Egypt" (Jeremiah 24:1b–4, 8, NIV). Having one time ill advisedly taken figs in my luggage from the Middle East to England, I have a firsthand experience of what bad figs are.

Another example of judgment associated with figs is from the life of Jesus. The only thing Jesus cursed in His lifetime was a fig tree: "In the morning, as they went along, they saw the fig tree withered from the roots. Peter remembered and said to Jesus, 'Rabbi, look! The fig tree you cursed has withered!'" (Mark 11:20–21, NIV).

The common fig, *Ficus carica*, is the most widely planted fruit tree in Bible lands. The tree lives up to 200 years, so is often planted with olive trees, which are also long lived. It is a many-branched tree, with the branches rising from low on the trunk. All parts of the tree contain a white, milky sap, which can cause dermatitis in sensitive individuals. Leaves are about the size of a hand and have three main lobes and a hairy undersurface.

The fig is the last tree in the Middle East to produce leaves in the spring. While the leaves of almond and other deciduous trees are fully developed, the fig is just beginning to leaf out. Jesus refers to this fact: "Take the fig tree as a parable: as soon as its twigs grow supple and its leaves come out, you know that summer is near. So with you, when you see these things happening: know that he is near, right at the gates" (Mark 13:28–29, NJB). This verse about the beginning of summer is often used to interpret Bible prophecies.

The best known fig leaves may be those used to cover the nakedness of Adam and Eve in the Garden of Eden: "At that moment their eyes were opened, and they suddenly felt shame at their nakedness. So they sewed fig leaves together to cover themselves" (Genesis 3:7, NLT). Fig leaves may be conspicuous, but fig flowers are nondescript.

Undersurface of fig leaf
with developing figs,
in May, near Saladin
Citadel, northern Syria.

Fig in March in
northern Galilee,
Israel. The syconia
(which contain the
flowers) are developing
and the leaves have
not yet emerged.

Why does Jesus not ask his disciples to look for the flowers of the fig? Because they are not seen by the casual observer. More than once when lecturing to Middle East audiences, I have asked how many have seen flowers of figs. Most often the response is that figs do not have flowers! The flowers of the fig are so furtive that even the farmers who grow the figs have not seen them. The uncolored, unisexual flowers are contained in a specialized, fleshy structure termed a syconium, or fig. Wild fig trees, known as caprifigs, have many female flowers and few male ones. The cultivated fig tree has only female flowers.

How do the sexes meet? This process is among the wonders of nature. A minute wasp, barely discernible to the naked eye, deposits eggs in the flowers of the caprifig and turns these flowers into galls—hard, inedible structures. The female wasps that develop from the galls are fertilized by the males while still in the flower, and leave the syconium through a small opening at the top of the fig. On the way out, the wasps must pass the male flowers and are dusted with pollen.

Free from the fig in which they were born, the female wasps then carry pollen to the female flower to effect fertilization. Because the egg-depositing structures of the wasps are too short, they cannot deposit eggs in the ovaries of the cultivated fig; while in the wild fig, the ovaries are within reach and therefore are turned into galls yielding inedible fruits. Fruit production in the fig is thus totally dependent on the wasp as a carrier of the pollen from the male figs. But modern varieties of fig trees can produce delicious fruit independent of wasp pollination.

Technically, the fruit is not a true fruit but rather a multiple fruit: each of the tiny fig flowers develops into a separate fruit, and these hundreds of tiny fruits together produce the fruit we call a fig.

If figs are not pollinated, they turn brown and fall from the tree. This may account for the biblical image in Isaiah: "All the stars of the heavens will be dissolved and the sky rolled up like a scroll; all the starry host will fall like withered leaves from the vine, like shriveled figs from the fig tree" (Isaiah 34:4, NIV).

The chief ancient use of the fig was for its fruit, as we read in the divine commentary on the tree: "The fig tree replied, 'Must I forgo my sweetness, forgo my excellent fruit, to go and sway over the trees?'" (Judges 9:11, NJB). In the case of King Hezekiah, figs were used medicinally as a poultice: "Isaiah had said, 'Prepare a poultice of figs and put it on the boil so he may recover'" (Isaiah 38:21; II Kings 20:7, MSG).

A fig tree may produce several crops in one year. There are many different varieties of figs: some with black fruits, some green, some red. Because the fig contains a high concentration of sugar, the fruits can be dried and stored for later use, a practice referred to several places in the Bible (I Samuel 25:18, 30:11–12).

The fig is often associated with grapes and is one of the "six species of the land" (Deuteronomy 8:8). Blessing for Israel is often symbolized by the prosperity of the grape and the fig together (I Kings 4:25; Micah 4:4; Zechariah 3:10).

Luscious green, black, red, or yellow fruits belie the furtive nature of the sex lives of figs. The flowers are never exposed, and pollination takes place within a special chamber. Perhaps this is the reason that the fig is sometimes associated with eschatology. On the other hand, it is also clearly presented for what it is—a common, easily grown tree with a delicious fruit.

Flax

Closeup of flax flowers in November, near Solay, Ethiopia.

FLAX WAS THE MOST IMPORTANT plant fiber in Bible times. It was the source of linen, and cloth was made either from linen or wool. While its production has declined in recent years because of the superiority of cotton, a softer fiber more readily handled by machines, flax remains one of the most important fiber plants in the world because of the long, strong fibers found in the outer layers of the stem.

In processing, the outer layers of the stem are removed by a kind of controlled decay called "retting." Retting in drier climates is accomplished by allowing the cut stalks of flax to remain out in the dew until the fiber-containing layers separate from the stem. This is probably why Rahab had bundles of flax on her roof: "But she had brought them [the spies] up to the roof and hidden them with the stalks of flax, which she had laid in order on the roof" (Joshua 2:6, NKJV). After retting, the fibers are cleaned and then bleached in the sun. Then the fibers are separated and woven into wicks or cords or spun into cloth. The linen produced in Egypt was especially fine: "And workers in flax will be in despair, and the carders and those at the loom will grow pale. Its weavers will be dismayed, and all who work for wages will be grieved" (Isaiah 19:9–10, ASV).

The scientific name of flax is *Linum usitatissimum*. The term *usitatissimum* means "most useful," a suitable appellation for a plant used for both food and fiber. Flax is sown in the winter in the Middle East and

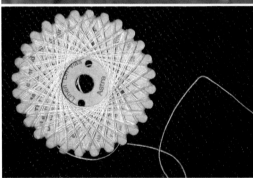

Traditional flax culture in November, Oromia State, Ethiopia. This flax is grown for the seeds, which are an important food source. One way flax is eaten is to roast the seeds, then grind them and mix with milk.

Linen is derived from the stem of the flax. The long, strong flax fibers are made into linen.

flowers in the late spring. With sky-blue flowers that open only in the morning, flax is among the most beautiful of all crops when flowering; it is often planted as an ornamental.

Linen had several uses in Bible times. The primary use was for clothing, but in cord form it was also used as wicks and measuring lines: "A bruised reed shall he not break, And smoking flax shall he not quench, Till he send forth judgment unto victory" (Matthew 12:20, ASV, based on Isaiah 42:3); and, "He had a flax cord and a measuring rod in his hand and was standing in the gateway" (Ezekiel 40:3b, NJB). The English word "line" is from the Latin word for flax, *linum*. Words such as linear and lineage also derive from the same linguistic root.

One use of flax that is not mentioned in the Bible is culinary. Flax seeds are among the oldest known foods, and are often found with barley and wheat in archaeological sites throughout the Middle East (Zohary and Hopf 2000). Linseed oil is expressed from the seeds of flax.

In many years working in the Middle East, I have never seen flax growing, which is remarkable since it evolved in this region (Zohary and Hopf 2000). I learned that flax is not well known among local farmers, in an experience at the regional office of agriculture of the Palestinian National Authority in Tubas (the ancient Thebez of the Bible), a region of intensive farming. One of my former students was the local agricultural officer. He asked me to try to identify some seeds recovered by police from a man arrested and incarcerated on charges of growing a drug plant. The seeds were flax! While a host of compounds are present in flax, many that are beneficial for health, no narcotics have been identified (Oomah 2001).

Flower of the Field

Poppy, *Papaver rhoeas,*
flower opening, near
Ajlon, Jordan

SPRING IN THE HOLY LAND COMES early. By February, the hills above the Jordan Valley and elsewhere are filled with riotous masses of wildflowers in a spectacular display. In fact, the hills above the Ghor, the Jordan Valley, have one of the most diverse floras per unit area on our planet. A plant that particularly stands out here is the red poppy.

This poppy may be the plant referred to by the Apostle Peter: "All men are like grass, and all their glory is like the flowers of the field; the grass withers and the flowers fall" (I Peter 1:24, NIV). This fleeting bloom is probably the common poppy, *Papaver rhoeas.*

Each poppy plant has a single flower that rises from a prominent bud. Poppies are distinctive in having petals crinkled in the bud, resembling crepe paper. As they open, they smooth out, and within a day, fall off the plant, leaving the ground littered with petals that soon dry and lose their color in the hot sun. Poppy fruits contain abundant small seeds dispensed through numerous pores.

Superficially, poppy may be confused with the common anemone, *Anemone coronaria.* However, the poppy is annual, while the anemone is perennial.

The Quran likens the brevity of life to a field that soon turns to stubble: "Present to them the example of the life of this world so like the water We send down from the skies that mingles with the earth

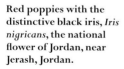

Red poppies with the distinctive black iris, *Iris nigricans*, the national flower of Jordan, near Jerash, Jordan.

The poppy flower remains open for less than a day and by evening the petals are gone. Jebel Abdel Aziz, northern Mesopotamia, Syria, in May.

The capsule of the poppy has a distinctive "salt shaker" construction. Sair, near Hebron, in May.

to nourish its vegetation, which then on the morrow turns to stubble and is blown away by the wind. God has power over every thing" (Sura 18:45, Ali). The rich man had boasted to his poorer neighbor, only to find that it was all in vain when God was left out.

Thus in both holy books, the fleeting nature of human life is likened to the vegetation that is vibrant one day but soon passes. Only what is eternal will last.

Frankincense

High-quality frankincense purchased in Omdurman, Sudan.

ANY SUNDAY SCHOOL CHRISTMAS program is likely to mention the gifts of the magi: gold, frankincense, and myrrh. So frankincense is a readily recognized Bible term.

Frankincense is prepared from the gum of several species of *Boswellia* (Burseraceae), trees and shrubs native to the Arabian Peninsula and North Africa. Incense is obtained from the gummy resin that can naturally exude from the plant, but usually cuts are made to stimulate oozing. Milky at first, the resin dries into translucent, amber-colored, hard drops that are harvested several weeks after oozing to the surface of the plant.

The word "frankincense" is derived from two words meaning "high-quality incense"; it is best known for burning as incense. The fragrance reminds me somewhat of pine resin. Widely used in the ancient Middle East, frankincense would have been known in the Arabian Peninsula though it is not included in the Quran. In the Bible, on the other hand, incense is mentioned about 140 times. Frankincense was an essential ingredient in the holy incense required for worship in the Old Testament.

The formula is given in Exodus: "Then the LORD said to Moses, 'Take fragrant spices—gum resin, onycha and galbanum—and pure frankincense, all in equal amounts, and make a fragrant blend of incense, the work of a perfumer. It is to be salted and pure and sacred' " (Exodus 30:34–35, NIV). Salt was added for unknown reasons.

Three *Boswellia papyrifera* trees on a ridge in Tigray Province, Ethiopia, in October. The trees have lost most of their leaves as the dry season approaches.

Villager bruising bark of frankincense tree to induce exudation of sap, in October, Tigray Province, Ethiopia.

Milky latex exuding from broken frankincense stem. The latex is an oleoresin produced in the phloem tissue of the tree. Tigray Province, Ethiopia, in October.

Modern-day incense compounding still depends heavily on frankincense. The resin has several uses in addition to incense (Langenheim 2003)—in small quantities to flavor certain candies and baked goods and also as a medicine to stop bleeding. Frankincense is a common commodity in Middle East markets where incense is highly valued by local people.

Despite the demand for frankincense, all harvest is from native plants; it is not grown commercially. Because it is such a highly valued natural product in the region, its harvest has contributed to the reduction of tree and shrub populations.

Galbanum

Ferula **species, Platres, Cyprus, in May. The large, yellow mass of flowers is typical of this genus. Several species were used in ancient times for their putative medicinal value.**

GALBANUM IS ONE OF THE MOST mysterious plant products in the Bible; its true identity remains elusive. Most Bible plant scholars have suggested that it is a species of *Ferula*, a member of the same family as carrot and parsley. There are several species of that genus in the flora of the Middle East (Post 1903).

The sole biblical reference to galbanum regards compounding incense: "Take sweet spices: storax, onycha, galbanum, sweet spices and pure frankincense in equal parts" (Exodus 30:34b, NJB).

All species of *Ferula* are herbaceous plants, often with very large leaves and masses of small yellow flowers. The entire plant contains a resin that is often pleasantly scented. Plants are valued for their use in food. The spice asofoetida, especially prominent in Indian cuisine, is derived from *Ferula assa-foetida*. Today, some species of *Ferula* are important in the perfume industry, and there is evidence that the plant was used for that purpose in ancient times as well.

Within the past 20 years, *Ferula hermonis* (the specific epithet refers to Mount Hermon, where it is known to grow) was reported to be an aphrodisiac. This belief led to extreme overharvesting of the native plant, so that a few years ago I was unable to find it on the Syrian part of the mountain. There is overwhelming scientific evidence that there is no basis for this putative value, but the plant still remains of interest among local people.

Gall

The purple blotches on the stem of poison hemlock give the plant its specific epithet *maculatum*, or spotted.

DARKNESS, MYSTERY, SUFFERING, bitterness—these are some of the images that we conjure up when we think of wormwood, hemlock, and gall. Are these plants? Products of plants?

Gall, as mentioned in the scriptures, has been translated from several words and in several ways: "He shall flee from the iron weapon, and the bow of steel shall strike him through. It is drawn, and cometh out of the body; yea, the glittering sword cometh out of his gall: terrors are upon him" (Job 20:25, KJV). In that verse, the Hebrew word *mererah* refers to the bodily fluid gall. In the same chapter, the word is used to indicate the venom of a poisonous snake (Job 20:24–25, KJV).

The word *rowsh* is also used for a weed: "And so-called justice spreads like a poisonous weed along the furrows of the fields!" (Hosea 10:4, NJB). In fact, in most cases *rowsh* is likely the product of a plant, as implied through its association with other plants: "Make sure there is no root among you that produces such bitter poison" (Deuteronomy 29:18b, NIV); and, "Their grapes are filled with poison, and their clusters with bitterness" (32:32b, NIV). The next verse in Deuteronomy (32:33) uses a different word for the poison of serpents.

Further evidence linking gall (*rowsh*) with a plant or plant product occurs in the two references where gall and wormwood are mentioned together: "Make sure there is no man or woman, clan or tribe among you today whose heart turns away from the Lord our God to go and worship the gods of those nations; make sure there is no root among

Poison hemlock (*Conium maculatum*) plants about 3 meters (10 feet) tall, in May, along an irrigation ditch near Antakya (biblical Antioch), Turkey. Poison hemlock occurs over a large area of North America in similar wet habitats.

Immature capsule of opium poppy, *Papaver somniferum*. I incised the capsule so the latex could exude.

you that produces such bitter poison [*rowsh*]" (Deuteronomy 29:18, NJB).

In the New Testament, gall is mentioned in only two verses: "For I perceive that thou art in the gall of bitterness, and in the bond of iniquity" (Acts 8:23, KJV, where the Greek *chole* is translated as "bitterness"); and, "They gave him wine to drink mixed with gall, which he tasted but refused to drink" (Matthew 27:34, NJB, where it is translated "gall").

Which plant fits the characteristics of gall? It must be both bitter and toxic. According to the New Testament account, it might have a narcotic affect. We can also assume that it is a plant familiar to readers of the original text.

Bitterness is widespread in plants. Many common plants like oak can be bitter. Bitterness can be a means of protecting the plant from grazing or, in more specialized cases, from predation by certain insects. Many plants in the indigenous flora of western Asia are toxic. One plant, however, stands out in its toxicity—poison hemlock (*Conium maculatum*). (Poison hemlock should not be confused with the common tree known in English as hemlock (*Tsuga*), which is not toxic and is used to make the original root beer. Early European settlers in North America likened the appearance of the hemlock tree's leaves to the poisonous plant, freighting this innocuous tree with a frightening name.) Poison hemlock is widespread in the Middle East and Europe, and has been introduced to North America.

Poison hemlock is an herbaceous plant that flowers in the spring and prefers moist habitats. It is common along irrigation ditches. It has many heads consisting of masses of small, white flowers similar to those of the wild carrot (Queen Anne's lace, *Daucus carota*), a common weed. Stems have distinctive purple mottling, hence the Latin specific epithet *maculatum*, meaning mottled. Leaves bear a resemblance to the common carrot (also *Daucus carota*). The single-seeded fruits ("seeds") resemble those of carrot, caraway, and cumin, all members of Apiaceae or the carrot family. Because of the resemblance of its fruit and odor to other members of the carrot family, poison hemlock has been accidentally ingested by humans and grazing animals, sometimes with fatal results.

Further supporting evidence that hemlock could be the gall of the Bible is its long history of use, well documented in ancient times. Perhaps the best-known reference is the suicide of Socrates, who drank hemlock. In the description of his dying, he notes losing the feeling in his feet and his hands. This reaction is due to the effect of coniine, a central nervous system poison.

Zohary (1982) suggests that an alternative to hemlock is a group of often toxic plants related to tobacco and tomato—species of the genus *Hyoscyamus*, most of which grow in very dry areas. One, *Hyoscyamus reticulatus*, can be found at the margins of fields in western Asia but at a very low frequency.

A less likely plant for gall is the opium poppy, *Papaver somniferum*, which is apparently not native in Bible lands. Growth of this species in ancient Egypt has not been unequivocally documented (de Vartavan and Amorós 1997). It is sometimes planted as an ornamental in Syria. The fresh latex of this plant is very bitter.

The emphasis in the use and application of gall is its extremely unpleasant taste and poisonous nature. Several plants fit this category, though hemlock, a widespread and common poison plant, is a sturdy candidate.

Garlic

Garlic has an ancient history.

REGARDING GARLIC, BOTH THE Quran and the Bible refer to the same incident—when people complained to Moses about food as they traveled in the wilderness: "O Moses, we are tired of eating the same food, ask your Lord to give us fruits of the earth, herbs and cucumbers, grains and lentils and onions" (Sura 2:61, Ali); and, "We remember the fish that we ate in Egypt for nothing; the cucumbers, and the melons, and the leeks, and the onions, and the garlic" (Numbers 11:5, JND). Any visitor to Egypt knows that garlic, *Allium sativum*, is still one of the most widely used flavorings in food in that country.

Garlic is linked with onion, both in the scriptures and in grocery stores, but there are significant differences in their biology. First, garlic is sterile and must be planted from bulbs. The structure of the bulb is much different in onion and garlic. The onion bulb consists of overlapping scale leaves while the garlic bulb is formed from the thickened leaf bases that develop within a common covering. There is considerable evidence that garlic was widespread in the ancient Middle East (Mathew 1996, Zohary and Hopf 2000).

Garlic is an example of a *hapax legomenon*, a Greek term for something mentioned only once, in the Bible. This fact is striking, since garlic was used extensively at the time the biblical verse was written. And further evidence is provided by the ubiquitous traditional use of garlic today in foods of the entire Mediterranean region.

Garlic drying
in a window in
Hama, Syria.

Field of garlic
in February, in
Wadi Jhhanem,
Lebanon. The bulbs
were planted in
the winter and
will be harvested
in the spring.

Ginger

Ginger flavors a drink in Paradise.

THE ONLY CLEARLY IDENTIFIABLE plant included in the Quran but not in the Bible is ginger, one of the oldest, best-known spices. In fact, ginger (*Zingiber officinale*) has been in cultivation so long that it is unknown in the wild. Familiar to many as a component of soft drinks like ginger ale, ginger has become more generally popular with increased interest in Asian food. The Quran mentions it as a drink in a description of Paradise: "They shall be served on silver dishes, and beakers as large as goblets; silver goblets which they themselves shall measure; and cups brim-full with ginger-flavored water from a fountain called Salsibil" (Sura 76:15–18, Dawood).

Miller (1969) points out that ginger, as well as the Arabic cognate *zanjabil*, are derived from a Sanskrit word for the spice, attesting to the antiquity of this pungent condiment. The name of the fountain, Salsibil, is also derived from the word for ginger.

Ginger is tropical and grown in many regions of the world. We use the rhizome, which is harvested after the leaves die back. The rhizome can be eaten fresh, and is frequently dried for preservation, powdered, and used for distillation of volatiles for the flavor industry.

The same caravans that brought ginger to Arabia could have brought it to Palestine. Yet it is not mentioned in the Bible. Whatever the reason, ginger was highly valued in Arabia. Perhaps that is why it is mentioned as a drink in Paradise.

Field of ginger in Sri Lanka ready for harvest. The leaves and above-ground stems have died back and the rhizomes are being dug. Ginger from South Asia was widely marketed in ancient times.

Ginger, Sri Lanka. Much of the local ginger in Sri Lanka is eaten fresh.

Gourd

Gourd flower and leaves.

THE GOURD, MORE ACCURATELY termed the colycinth, *Citrullus colocynthis*, is a common herbaceous vine found in dry areas. Colycinth is different from the multicolored ornamental gourds, *Cucurbita pepo* subspecies *ovifera*. Instead, it is related to watermelon, which it resembles in many ways. Colycinth creeps along the ground and has dissected leaves. The fruit is about the size of an orange, with a yellowish rind, greenish pulp, and light brown seeds. Fruits are attractive, deceptively so. Foolishly, I tasted the pulp of the fruit and had a numb tongue for several hours. The taste of the flesh is extremely bitter, but it is readily available from Arab herbalists as a medicine. This may be the bitter gourd in the Quran (Sura 34:16, Ali).

In II Kings 4:38–39, the sons of the prophets had to prepare a meal for a large group and apparently at short notice. One of Elisha's disciples went out into the field to get some food. As he was collecting various edible plants, he happened upon the colycinth (called "gourd" in the verse). The result was a memorable dinner party where the guests thought they were being poisoned.

Gourds were used ornamentally in Solomon's temple (I Kings 6:18a). They were also depicted as ornamental objects in several famous Byzantine mosaics in Jordan (Piccirillo 1992).

Flowering and fruiting gourd in March, in the Negev, Israel. The fruits remained on the vine from the previous season.

Broken pieces of gourd sold in an herbalist's shop in Amman. Considered a panacea for several digestive ailments, gourd's bitter flavor no doubt enhances the lore of the remedy.

Grape

The white grape variety *salti* is a popular table grape among Palestinians. In July, Kufur Yusef, Galilee.

N
O PLANT IS MENTIONED MORE times in the Bible than grape, *Vitis vinifera*, and its products, chiefly wine (200 times) but also grapes (50 times), raisins, syrup, and vinegar. In contrast, the Quran has only eight references to grape.

In Bible times, the grape vine was grown solely for its fruit. Even the wood of the vine was considered worthless: "The word of the LORD came to me: 'Son of man, how is the wood of a vine better than that of a branch on any of the trees in the forest? Is wood ever taken from it to make anything useful? Do they make pegs from it to hang things on? And after it is thrown on the fire as fuel and the fire burns both ends and chars the middle, is it then useful for anything? If it was not useful for anything when it was whole, how much less can it be made into something useful when the fire has burned it and it is charred?' " (Ezekiel 15:1–5, NIV).

A woody vine with tendrils, *Vitis vinifera* is native to the Middle East and to the whole Mediterranean region, and it is not easy to discern whether the grape still occurs wild in nature (Zohary and Hopf 2000). Other species of grape are found in different parts of the world including North America. If left alone, grape will climb and expend much of its energy into creating branches. Pruning of this growth is essential for the vine to produce grapes. This process is referred to in several scriptures: "I shall let it [the grapevine] go to waste, unpruned, undug, overgrown by brambles and thorn-bushes" (Isaiah 5:6, NJB);

My friend Abu
Wadiah pruning
grapes in Cana,
in Galilee, Israel.
Grape is more
accurately termed
"wine grape"
(*Vitis vinifera*).

Inflorescence
of grape flowers
in May, at Sair,
near Hebron.

and, "I [Jesus] am the true vine, and my father is the vine dresser. Every branch in me that bears no fruit he cuts away, and every branch that does bear fruit he prunes to make it bear even more" (John 15:1–2, NJB).

Vineyards in the Bible are often hedged with piles of fieldstones or stone walls. The flowers of the grape are greenish and inconspicuous, but they are very fragrant: "The fig trees are forming young fruit, and the fragrant grapevines are blossoming. Rise up, my darling! Come away with me, my fair one!" (Song of Solomon 2:13, NLT). The grape is especially vulnerable to damage at the flowering stage. If flowers do not develop, there will be no fruit. In addition to late frosts at higher altitudes, animals can cause damage.

Foxes, which feed on grapes, are common in the Middle East; at least three species occur. One species is so secretive that its presence in Israel was discovered only a few years ago. These sly creatures are usually nocturnal in their behavior. In parts of Galilee, it is possible to hear them at night—their haunting howls coming from the forests and vineyards. Foxes are slight animals, about the size of a small dog. Their agility is mentioned in Nehemiah 4:3, where Tobiah, with sarcasm, suggests that the lightest animal would break down the wall. They can climb up even the smallest vines, and modern farmers still consider them a menace in vineyards.

The spreading, climbing character of the grapevine is mentioned positively in the Bible: "Joseph is a fruitful vine, a fruitful vine near a spring, whose branches climb over a wall" (Genesis 49:22, NIV). The image is also used in a negative sense: "Israel was a luxuriant vine yielding plenty of fruit. The more his fruit increased, the more altars he built; the richer his land became, the richer he made the sacred pillars" (Hosea 10:1, NJB).

In areas with low moisture, grapevines are often allowed to grow on the soil surface. Vineyards of this type are still found near Hebron (not far from the Valley of Eschol, of Numbers 13:23), as well as other dry areas suitable for grapes, such as the Hauran region of Syria.

Shallow plowing of a
vineyard near Suweida,
Syria. Plowing and weeding
the vineyard reduces pests
and also allows the soil
to remain dry from dew
while the grapes mature.

I visited a friend's large vineyard at Mamre near Hebron. It was in August, just as the grapes were beginning to ripen. The rains had stopped in April, so the surrounding hills were dry and brown, setting the deep green of the vine leaves in sharp relief. Some of the vines we examined were more than a century old, with large, gnarled stems contrasting with the delicate, well-tended branches.

Wine (made from grapes) is closely associated with Christian worship through the communion service. The Quran refers to "rivers of wine delectable to drinkers" in Paradise (Sura 47:15, Ali).

Wine is the best-known product of grapes because the high sugar content of the berries allows for fermentation. The yeasts that become attached to the waxy covering of the berries facilitate fermentation. Producing wine is a way to preserve the product of the grape indefinitely. A syrup is often made from grape juice which is used in preparing a special kind of candy, most popular in Aleppo. To prepare the candy, walnuts are tied on a string at regular intervals. The string is then repeatedly dipped in the grape syrup until the nut and the string are covered. The long, brown strings are hung in the market, for purchase.

Vinegar is a Bible food product produced from wine. After fermentation, bacteria change the alcohol to acetic acid. Another familiar product of grapes is raisins (dried grapes). For this use, seedless varieties of grape are best. Less known is a preparation from the unripe, green grapes (using either green or red varieties of grapes) used as flavoring for food. When the grape is hard and green (usually in May in the Middle East), it is picked and dried. After drying, it is ground and stored. I have not seen this product commercially produced, but several Arab friends have given me the homemade powder. It adds a pleasant sourness to food.

In addition to wine, the Bible mentions two other uses for grapes and suggests a third. The sour nature of immature grapes is noted: "What mean ye, that ye use this proverb concerning the land of Israel, saying, 'The fathers have eaten sour grapes, and the children's teeth are set on edge?'" (Ezekiel 18:1–2, KJV); and, "For afore the harvest, when the bud is perfect, and the sour grape is ripening in the flower, he shall both cut off the sprigs with pruning hooks, and take away and cut down the branches" (Isaiah 18:5, KJV).

Grape leaves are also used for food. They are considered a delicacy by Arabs for preparation of a dish in which rice flavored with meat and spices is wrapped in young grape leaves—a use not specifically mentioned in the Bible. The grape leaves are pleasantly sour. This dish is made in different versions throughout the Mediterranean region.

Figs and grapes are often mentioned together in the Bible (I Kings 4:25; II Kings 18:31). The fruits of both plants develop about the same time in midsummer. The grape harvest and the winepress are often associated in the Bible with judgment: "Then another Angel came out of the Temple in Heaven. He also had a sharp sickle. Yet another Angel, the one in charge of tending the fire, came from the Altar. He thundered to the Angel who held the sharp sickle, 'Swing your sharp sickle. Harvest earth's vineyard. The grapes are bursting with ripeness'" (Revelation 14:17–18, MSG).

Perhaps no single plant is more closely associated with the life and ministry of Jesus than the grape. His first miracle was turning water into wine, and he referred to himself as the "true vine." The strength of this imagery can hardly be overemphasized in studying the scripture: it demonstrates the intimate relationship between viticulture in Jesus's day and the manner in which he used it in his teaching. Grapes remain one of the most important fruit crops in western Asia.

Henna

I purchased this henna powder in a shop in Ramallah.

HENNA EXTRACTS ARE NOW COMmon in various cosmetics, particularly shampoos, continuing a traditional use for centuries.

Henna is a many-branched shrub that grows to a height of about 3 meters (12 feet). Leaves are small and elliptic. The individual flowers, borne in the spring, are small but produced in large masses and are very fragrant. The dried flowers retain the heavy scent. Today henna is often grown as an ornamental.

The henna plant, *Lawsonia inermis*, is probably native to North Africa but may have been grown in hot oases such as Ein Gedi. This beautiful oasis sits between the Dead Sea and the precipitous cliffs of the Judean Desert and is a place where many medicinal and cosmetic plants were grown in ancient times. The climate is tropical and there is an abundant supply of water. The Bible offers a sensuous allusion to henna and the oasis: "My beloved is unto me a cluster of henna flowers in the vineyards of Ein Gedi" (Song of Solomon 1:14, NIV). The intense fragrance of the henna is also suggested in Songs of Songs 4:13, where it is mentioned with spikenard, probably *Nardostachys jatamansi*.

The main use of henna is as a cosmetic. Today the highest quality henna in the Middle East is imported from Iran. The leaves are dried and crushed into a fine powder. This powder is mixed with water and allowed to sit for two days to make a paste that forms a reddish dye,

Flowers on an ornamental henna plant in a Jericho garden.

A bride adorned with henna designs performing the traditional "pigeon dance" at a Sudanese wedding. In Sudan and some other countries, the extent of henna application on wedding guests is in proportion to relationship with the bride or groom. A sister may have one arm or both arms adorned. As a guest but not a family member, I was invited to have my thumb stained. Photo by Libby Musselman.

which is then painted on the fingernails, hands, and feet as ornamentation, often with intricate designs. Henna is also used to dye the hair. While it is used in several countries, I have seen henna most widely applied in Sudan, especially to adorn the bride at a wedding.

In Bible days, cosmetic use of henna may have been even more widespread. There is a reference in Deuteronomy 21:12, which may allude to the need for the colored hair and nails to grow out. While henna was certainly used in ancient times as a cosmetic, the only reference to it in the scriptures relates to the plant's fragrant flowers.

Hyssop

Hyssop flowers in June, near Kufur Sumei, Galilee, Israel.

H YSSOP IS ONE OF THE BETTER-
known plants of the Bible: it is
referred to in 10 places in the Old
Testament and two places in the New Testament. It is not mentioned in the Quran.

This plant, or a product of this plant, formed an important part of Passover: "Take a bunch of hyssop, dip it into the blood in the basin and put some of the blood on the top and on both sides of the door-frame" (Exodus 12:22a, NIV); for ceremonial cleansing of skin disease (Leviticus 14:4); and regarding the red heifer offering: "The priest is to take some cedar wood, hyssop and scarlet wool and throw them onto the burning heifer" (Numbers 19:6, NIV). David mentions hyssop in the Psalms, perhaps in regard to the Numbers sacrifice: "Purge me with hyssop, and I shall be clean: wash me, and I shall be whiter than snow" (Psalm 51:7, KJV).

In the New Testament, Hebrews 9:19 refers to the ceremonial cleansing of the Children of Israel and the use of hyssop. Interestingly, hyssop is not specifically mentioned for this incident in the Old Testament. Another reference, I Kings 4:33, is the only Old Testament verse that does not mention hyssop in a ceremonial use. It is also one of the most puzzling verses dealing with hyssop.

According to Bible verses, hyssop (*ezov* in Hebrew) has certain features. It can grow on a "wall": "He [Solomon] described plant life,

Hyssop growing near Kufur Yusef, Galilee, Israel, in March. This plant is ready for harvest. As with any native plant, the concentration of flavoring compounds is variable. Therefore, there has been an effort to select flavorful plants for commercial production.

Local people in Northern Galilee harvest hyssop in nature in May. Each household may have a distinct recipe for preparing it as a spice.

from the cedar of Lebanon to the hyssop that grows out of walls" (I Kings 4:33a, NIV). The plant and its extracts are useful for purgatives: in both Leviticus 14 and Numbers 19, hyssop is associated with cedar wood, implying a purgative application. Moreover, hyssop may have been commercially available perhaps in the same way it is today.

For all of these uses, *Origanum syriacum*, a plant known in English as Syrian hyssop and a relative of the well-known kitchen herbs oregano and marjoram, seems the most likely candidate for the hyssop of the Bible. Hyssop does not grow in Egypt nor is it recorded from any archaeological finds (de Vartavan and Amorós 1997), though it has been found growing in Sinai (Fleisher and Fleisher 1988).

Modern Bible scholars still express uncertainty about the actual identity of hyssop, and some suggest that it could be caper (*Capparis spinosa*), a common shrub in the Middle East (Moldenke and Moldenke 1952). The only evidence for this possibility is the verse in I Kings 4 that refers to hyssop (*ezov*) growing from a wall. The wall has often been assumed to be of masonry, similar to walls in the older parts of cities in the Middle East and on which caper is commonly seen growing. This interpretation, however, does not fit *Origanum syriacum*, since it does not grow out of stone walls. To suggest, however, that Solomon was thinking of caper, only complicates the matter, since caper in Hebrew is a different word, *ab'ionah*.

Another issue with caper is how it is used. The fruit, a soft berry-like structure when mature, was apparently used as an aphrodisiac. Since caper is armed and the leaves are waxy, it would not be suitable as an applicator as required in the Exodus 12 account. Palestinians I have interviewed do not use any part of the caper plant as a food or condiment.

Hyssop, *Origanum syriacum*, known in Arabic as *za'atar*, on the other hand, is one of the most widely used and valued herbs in the Middle East. A typical Arab breakfast is bread dipped in olive oil and *za'atar*. The leaves are available in dried form in Arab markets as a mixture of hyssop, sesame seeds, salt, and sometimes olive oil and other ingredients. The flavor is rather like that of pizza. I asked the Samaritans, native Arabic speakers, on Mount Gerizim, which plant they use for sprinkling in their Passover rites, and their answer was *za'atar*.

Add another issue to the pot: in I Kings 4:33, the Hebrew word *qir*, which has been translated as "wall," is worth examining. The word is often used to mean "wall" (Leviticus 14:37; I Kings 6:5), but that does not preclude the possibility that the word, in I Kings, refers to natural ledges that are common in the mountains. In this verse, Solomon is speaking of natural history, not manmade objects, so a masonry wall would be out of context. Indeed *Origanum syriacum* frequents rocky ledges and outcrops in the mountains, natural formations that can reasonably be described as wall-like.

Another problem in deciphering the identity of hyssop remains, as indicated in the other New Testament verse: "A jar of wine vinegar was there, so they soaked a sponge in it, put the sponge on a stalk of the hyssop plant, and lifted it to Jesus's lips" (John 19:29, NIV). The word here is the same as that in Hebrews 9:19, and there seems little doubt that hyssop is meant. The problem is how the plant was used. First, the sponge was put on a long stalk of the hyssop plant, which is unlikely because of the small stature of hyssop; it would nearly be impossible to find a stem more than 1 meter (3 feet) long and even then stems often branch. The Greek words meaning "binding it to hyssop" might also suggest that the hyssop plant was a holder for the sponge—plausible because of the branching growth habit of the hyssop. But why this holder would be necessary is unclear.

Hyssop, then, was used in Bible times for worship. Today, it is a widely consumed herb, a use not mentioned in the Bible. The plant is another example of a member of the Middle East native flora finding a place in the scriptures as well as in kitchens of today.

Ivy

Ivy, *Hedera helix*, is mentioned only in the Apocrypha, though it played a major role in several civilizations in the Mediterranean. Here ivy is climbing a tree, attaching with the specialized roots that arise from the stem, in Norfolk, Virginia.

HOLLY AND IVY ARE WELL-KNOWN holiday symbols. It is surprising to learn, therefore, that in ancient times their use was proscribed by Jews and early Christians. This restriction was probably because of the association of holly and especially ivy with Greek gods (Baumann 1993) and with garlands for wreaths and crowns of Apollo, which was idolatry (Forster 1952).

"People [Jews] were driven by hard compulsion to take part in the monthly ritual meal commemorating the king's birthday; and when a feast of Dionysius occurred, they were forced to wear ivy wreaths and walk in the Dionysiac procession. A decree was issued at the instance of the people of Ptolemais for the neighbouring Greek cities, enforcing the same conduct on the Jews there, obliging them to share in the sacrificial meals, and ordering the execution of those who would not voluntarily conform to Greek customs. So it became clear that disaster was imminent" (II Maccabees 6:7–9, NJB). The mandatory wearing of ivy and the atrocities inflicted on the Jews compelled to participate in these events would be enough to render ivy an anathema.

Dislike of these plants was mitigated in the Middle Ages (Trapp 1958), so that today, ivy, and to a greater extent holly, are associated with Christmas and New Year celebrations.

Ivy on rock face on Mount Lebanon. Courtesy Houssam Shaiban.

The plant of the dictum against garlanding is the common English ivy, *Hedera helix*, widely distributed throughout the Mediterranean region and much of Europe (Metcalfe 2005). It is a woody vine with evergreen leaves and can often climb very high. I have seen it in mature mixed-hardwood forests in Lebanon and Syria, but it is not as common there as in Anatolia and on the Greek peninsula. In nature, ivy climbs up forest trees, firmly attaching itself to the supporting surface with specialized roots. The clasping nature of the vine has been used in literature as a symbol of cleaving to a person in affection. Ivy flowers appear late in the year, followed by a purple-black berry. English ivy is widely planted for its attractive evergreen leaves and for the fruits, which are nutritious food for birds.

Ladanum

Pink cistus, showing the abundant glandular hairs that cover the plant. These produce a sticky, fragrant resin that is the basis of ladanum.

ONE OF THE MOST BEAUTIFUL shrubs in the pine forests of the Middle East are species of *Cistus,* the source of the resin known as ladanum (or labdanum). This resin has an ancient heritage, being cited in the first book of the Bible, and it has a long history of use: "Then their father Israel [Jacob] said to them [Joseph's brothers], 'If it [the trip to Egypt] must be, then do this: Put some of the best products of the land in your bags and take them down to the man as a gift— a little balm and a little honey, some spices and myrrh [*lote*], some pistachio nuts and almonds'" (Genesis 43:11, NIV); and, "As they sat down to eat their meal, they looked up and saw a caravan of Ishmaelites coming from Gilead. Their camels were loaded with spices, balm and myrrh [*lote*], and they were on their way to take them down to Egypt" (Genesis 37:25, NIV). The Hebrew *lote* should not be confused with the Arabic *lote* (see "Thornbush").

The cargo of the Ishmaelites is of special interest to the ethnobotanist. It is unfortunate that the Hebrew word *lote* is translated as "myrrh" in these two verses, while in the remaining 11 occurrences in both KJV and NIV, myrrh is more accurately used for the Hebrew *mor.*

What is *lote*? One possibility is the resin of species of *Cistus*, a shrub common in the region east of the Jordan River known as Gilead. The meaning of the word in Hebrew implies something sticky, characteristic of this product.

Dibbeen National Forest, Jordan, in May. The dominant tree in the forest is the Aleppo pine, with conspicuous white cistus in the understory.

White cistus flowers in May, Dibbeen National Forest, Jordan. While both the white and pink cistus of the Middle East can produce resin, the highest quality comes from species in Greece.

Although a small area, Gilead is geologically and ecologically diverse, stretching from the margins of the Jordan Valley and the peaks along the Great Rift Valley to the edge of the *badia* (Arabic for steppe). In ancient times, parts of Gilead were covered with forests. These forests were the southernmost extension of the Mediterranean woodlands and the southern edge of the range of the Aleppo pine (*Pinus halepensis*).

Two species of *Cistus* are common in the pine forest, *C. creticus* and *C. salvifolius*. They are easily distinguished by their flower color. The large pink flowers of *C. creticus* and the slightly smaller but equally beautiful white flowers of *C. salvifolius* appear in May. On a hot day, the fragrant resin of the plants is noticeable. On close examination, you can see the numerous hairs that cover the leaves and young stems of both species. The resinous ladanum will stick to your hands if you collect leaves (Langenheim 2003).

The fragrant resin of *Cistus* has been used for millennia to produce incense. The resin of related species is still collected in parts of Greece. It can be harvested in a variety of ways. One ancient method is to comb the hair of goats that graze in plant communities where *Cistus* is abundant. Another is by dragging a rake with long, leather tines across the shrubs at the hottest time of day, and when the resin is dry, removing it from the rake tines (Baumann 1993).

Like many other plants used for incense, ladanum has medicinal value. The resin is used as a balm to reduce inflammation of the skin. Recent research on the biochemistry of the plant has shown the efficacy of compounds in the plant for dermatological disorders (Danne et al. 1993), which may be due in part to the antimicrobial activity of compounds in the leaf (Demetzos et al. 1997, 1999). Research in Turkey shows that of the seven plants used as folk remedies for ulcers, the one with the greatest efficacy was *C. salvifolius* (Yesilada et al. 1999). Jacob's choice of ladanum, therefore, indicates the value placed by people of that time on this plant and its products and possibly reflects on the healing value of the resin.

To my knowledge, ladanum does not have any widespread use among modern Arabs. I have not found any local familiarity with the plants. When I encountered some Bedouin near Anjara, Jordan, feeding their sheep on *Cistus*, I asked how they used the plant. They simply replied that it was good forage for sheep and goats, and therefore the shrub is absent in heavily grazed areas.

Still used to compound incense in the Greek Orthodox Church, ladanum is a little-known product of an attractive flowering shrub of pine woodlands of the Middle East. While it is being examined for its diverse medicinal applications, local people generally are unaware of this or its use as incense. Ladanum bears no relation to laudanum, a tincture of opium that was a popular medicine in Victorian times.

Laurel

Fruiting laurel shrub near Kufur Sumei, Galilee, Israel.

AUREL WAS USED TO CROWN WIN-
ners in ancient games. It remains a winner today but in a different way. The
crowning use of laurel, *Laurus nobilis*, is still
for its leaves, known as bay leaves—not for
honor but to give an aromatic flavor to Mediterranean dishes. Laurel is a member of
the Lauraceae, a family known for aromatic
plants like cinnamon.

Two types of crowns are mentioned in the
New Testament. The first is a regal crown of
precious metal—what we would normally
think of as a crown. The second is the laurel
wreath that was presented to the winner of ancient games; the symbolism of this prize would be well known to New Testament writers acquainted with Greek culture. A kind of vegetable tiara, the laurel wreath was woven from the leaves and young branches of *Laurus
nobilis*. A literal translation of the Latin name is "noble laurel," an apt
description of this shrub or small tree that is common in forest communities throughout the Mediterranean region. Laurel is one of the
few plants mentioned solely in the New Testament.

Paul, the apostle, was strongly influenced by Greek culture, and the
laurel wreath of Greek games is implied in three of his epistles. The
wreath's image is especially clear in the following verse: "Similarly, if
anyone competes as an athlete, he does not receive the victor's crown
unless he competes according to the rules" (II Timothy 2:5, NIV).
And other apostles mention the laurel wreath. In one verse, a nonfad-
ing crown is contrasted with a fading laurel crown: "And when the

Laurel shrub near Kufur Sumei, Galilee, Israel. In the southern extent of its range (Jordan and Israel), laurel leaves are not used by local people, but the shrub is valued as fodder.

Chief Shepherd appears, you will receive the crown of glory that will never fade away" (I Peter 5:4, NIV). James suggests a laurel crown for those who withstand struggle: "Blessed is the man who perseveres under trial, because when he has stood the test, he will receive the crown of life that God has promised to those who love him" (James 1:12, NIV).

Laurel is a shrub or small tree with evergreen, leathery leaves. Like its relative sassafras, laurel is perfused with an aromatic oil. Flowers are greenish, small, and appear in the spring. Shiny, black, fleshy fruits are produced in October or November.

Best known today as the bay leaves of cooking, the tradition of laurel lives on in our language in such words as laureate and baccalaureate. The word "laurel" has been applied to a diversity of other plants that have a fragrance or flavor like *Laurus nobilis* (various types of bay leaves) or leaves resembling the plant.

Leek

Leek plants bundled for shipment to market using strands from the leaves of the date palm. In April, near Alexandria, Egypt.

MOST PLANTS MENTIONED AS foods in the Bible are still widely used in western Asia. Unique to the wilderness experience of the Children of Israel were five vegetables well known today—cucumbers, melons, leeks, onions, and garlic: "We remember the fish we used to eat for free in Egypt. And we had all the cucumbers, melons, leeks, onions, and garlic we wanted" (Numbers 11:5, NLT). Anyone who has spent time in the Middle East is aware how much all of these plants are relished, even considered essential, except for leeks.

The vegetable known as leek is generally regarded as *Allium porrum*. However, this plant is seldom grown in the Middle East. Leeks are available in larger cities but are purchased chiefly by foreigners. However, a kind of leek grown only in the Nile Delta of Egypt, known in Arabic as *kurrat* (*Allium kurrat*), is a well-known albeit minor crop.

There are several differences between *Allium porrum* and *A. kurrat*: *A. porrum* is larger, with a longer stem and a pronounced bulbous base (Jones and Mann 1963). *Allium porrum* is grown mainly for its white stems while *A. kurrat* is grown for its leaves. Leek and *kurrat* are closely related, with highly fertile hybrids (Kadry and Kamel 1959). And both *A. porrum* and *A. kurrat* are considered to be closely related to the widespread Mediterranean species, *A. ampeloprasum*; they are variously treated as varieties of that taxon or as separate taxa (Mathew 1996).

Remains of *kurrat* have been found at archaeological sites (Täckholm and Drar 1954, Murray 2000), indicating selection for this leafy type of leek from ancient times. But this species or cultivar of leek was not formally named until 1926, when K. Krause of the Dahlem Botanical Garden in Berlin found an allium flowering that had been grown from seeds collected by George Schweinfurth, who had spent many years botanizing in Egypt and Sudan.

Modern use of *kurrat* is in green salads and as a component of *tameeah*, the traditional fried cakes of broad beans (*Vicia faba*) so popular in Egypt. The leaves are not as stringy as those of *Allium porrum* (traditionally not eaten) but have a strong flavor (Musselman 2003).

Most English readers of the "vegetable list" in Numbers 11 envision the leeks mentioned there as the stout plants with a long white stem sold in grocery stores. The leeks in the Bible, though, were much shorter and lacked the larger stem.

Leek is common in the markets in Alexandria, Egypt, in the spring.

Field of leeks near Alexandria, Egypt. The leaves have been cut and the plants are allowed to resprout.

Lentil

The two main types of lentils in the Middle East: large, dark lentils and smaller, red lentils.

DUPED BY SOUP? JACOB, HAVING taken advantage of his brother through deceit, prepared a lentil soup: "Esau said to Jacob, 'Give me a mouthful of that red stuff there [lentil stew], I am exhausted'" (Genesis 25:30, 34, NJB).

In the Quran, the sole mention of lentils is in the "vegetable list" of Egyptian foods missed by the Children of Israel: "Remember, when you said: 'O Moses, we are tired of eating the same food (day after day), ask your Lord to give us fruits of the earth, herbs and cucumbers, grains and lentils and onions'" (Sura 2:61, Ali). In the same incident recorded in the Bible in Numbers 11:5, lentils are not mentioned.

Lentils, as in Bible days, are a significant food crop in the modern Middle East. Despite their widespread planting and use in a variety of dishes, the inclusion of this legume crop in the holy books is disproportionate to their importance and use. Lentils were among the most important crops in ancient Egypt (Murray 2000).

In addition to their inclusion in the story of Jacob and in the incident in the Quran, lentils are mentioned in II Samuel 17:28; II Samuel 23:11; and Ezekiel 4:9. *Lens culinaris*, lentils, were widely planted and utilized during Bible times. Like many other legumes, lentils are rich in essential amino acids, so they are a good supplement to a low-protein diet.

Lentil plants are low-growing, delicate annuals with small, white

Lentils grown in test plots at the International Center for Agricultural Research in the Dry Areas (ICARDA) near Aleppo, Syria. ICARDA is a world center for the study of lentils.

Fruits (legumes) of lentil. Each legume contains only a few seeds.

or bluish flowers. They are planted in the winter and are harvested in late spring or early summer, a cropping system that is the same as for barley and wheat. An interesting thing about the culture of lentils is that they are often grown in small patches. It is not uncommon to see a patch of lentils only a few meters (6 feet or more) in diameter among olive trees or on a ledge in the mountains.

Harvested lentil and barley are often taken to the same threshing floors because they ripen at the same time. These threshing floors in the region appear little changed since Bible days, with large flat rocks as a stone platform, worn smooth by centuries of threshing and surrounded by stone walls.

There are two main types of lentils in the Middle East. One is a large, dark lentil; this type is boiled and eaten without the seed coat removed. A common village food in the Middle East is a mixture of bulgur (*burghul* in Arabic) and lentils. The second is a small lentil with red cotyledons and a thick seed coat, which is usually prepared by grinding off the outer layer, the seed coat, leaving the red cotyledons. Lentils of this type cook more rapidly and are usually made into soups. The seed coat residue is fed to animals.

Widely grown, nutritious, and ancient, lentils are important throughout the Middle East. Little wonder that they are mentioned in both holy books.

Lily of the Field

Crimson-red form of lily of the field.

THE TYPICAL PRESENTATION OF this plant is in a picture of a smiling Jesus sitting with children on his lap in a grassy field with lily-like plants covering the ground. This common view is based on this verse: "And why do you worry about clothes? See how the lilies of the field grow. They do not labor or spin. Yet I tell you that not even Solomon in all his splendor was dressed like one of these. If that is how God clothes the grass of the field, which is here today and tomorrow is thrown into the fire, will he not much more clothe you, O you of little faith?" (Matthew 6:28–30, NIV). Though these lily-like plants are one of the best known in Bible lore, the plant is not a lily. It is unfortunate that it was translated as "lily." The image that most envision as a lily is the large trumpet-shaped flower of the common Easter lily (*Lilium candidum*), not a credible candidate for lily of the field.

Which plant Jesus is referring to is hard to say with certainty. The word translated "lily" here and in the parallel verses in Luke 12:27 is *krinon*. It is unlikely that a true lily, genus *Lilium*, is intended, because the one species native to the region, *Lilium candidum*, is restricted in its distribution. Rather, a more common plant widely known to local people is implied.

This plant has several characteristics. We know it is exceptionally colorful because of the allusion to Solomon's robes. Solomon was the most glorious of all the ancient kings of Israel so, consonant with

Vernal beauty in a field near
Suweida, Syria, in March .

Semitic literary hyperbole, this king was selected for mention in the verse. Second, it likely grows in a place where vegetation was harvested for burning, implying that it would not be an arid region where little herbage could be harvested.

Two widespread and beautiful native wildflowers fit these criteria. The first, and in my opinion the more probable, is the crown anemone, *Anemone coronaria*. This plant flowers from late winter (February) to early spring (April) in the Middle East, in open, sunny areas. Flowers are crimson red with a black center, and leaves are finely dissected and close to the ground. In some populations, the color of the flower may be purple or pink and rarely white. During the dry summer, leaves die back. With the advent of winter rains, the rhizome sprouts new leaves.

The common poppy, *Papaver rhoeas*, flower of the field, is a second candidate. Flowers of this annual plant last only one day, in contrast to the crown anemone, and by afternoon the petals have fallen off. While crown anemone and poppy may be found growing together, poppy is more frequent in drier areas. For this reason, it is unlikely (but not impossible) that vegetation would be harvested. A third possibility is that Jesus is not referring to a specific plant but simply pointing out the beauty of creation and God's care for it.

Mandrake

Mandrake fruits in May, near Amman, Jordan.

POSSIBLY NO BIBLE PLANT HAS THE aura of mystery of the mandrake, *Mandragora officinarum*. Although it is common throughout the Middle East, it is mentioned in the Bible in only two places and is absent in the Quran. Mandrake is a member of the nightshade family, which includes well-known poisonous plants such as nightshade, jimsonweed, and tobacco, as well as some common vegetables such as potato, tomato, green pepper, and eggplant.

The mandrake often grows as a weed in wheat fields: "Now in the days of wheat harvest Reuben went and found mandrakes in the field, and brought them to his mother Leah. Then Rachel said to Leah, 'Please give me some of your son's mandrakes'" (Genesis 30:14, NASB). The plant has several large, wrinkled, dark green leaves that lie flat on the ground in a rosette. In the center of the rosette, a cluster of attractive purple flowers appears in the winter. Flowers have hairs that prevent entry of water, an important adaptation for an urn-shaped flower that appears during the rainy season.

The fruits are produced in the early summer and have an attractive fragrance: "The mandrakes send out their fragrance, and at our door is every delicacy, both new and old, that I have stored up for you, my lover" (Song of Solomon 7:13, NIV) (Fleisher and Fleisher 1994). Mandrake fruits resemble a yellow cherry tomato. By the time the fruits are mature, the leaves of the mandrake and associated plants

Mandrake is a common weed in wheat fields that are not deeply plowed. Mandrake plant in wheat field in March, near Medaba, Jordan.

Mandrake plant in flower in December, near the village of Kufur Sumei, Upper Galilee, Israel.

have dried, awaiting winter rains. Arab friends warned me that the plant is toxic. On the other hand, Harrison (1956) states that local people eat it with impunity. So it was with some trepidation that I ate part of a ripe fruit. The taste was pleasant if somewhat insipid. If it is poisonous, then the poison is either weak or slow acting; I felt no discomfort after tasting the fruit.

The root of the mandrake may be 1 meter (3 feet) long and weigh several kilograms (about 4.5 pounds). It has bizarre, often human-like shapes, and for this reason is highly regarded by the superstitious.

Reuben was well advised to recommend the plant as a fertility drug. Recent research has shown that the plant has a rich diversity of active compounds, including some that might aid in conception.

Mint

Details of inflorescence of mint, near Jericho, in June. In common with other plants classified as herbs, the leaves of mint are used.

MINT IS MOST FREQUENTLY USED to flavor candy and drinks, while in the Middle East it is put in salads and cooked with meat as well. Perhaps it was used in similar ways in ancient times.

Mint, *Mentha longifolia*, and other species of *Mentha*, are native to the Middle East. The word *heduosmon* is translated "mint" in two Bible references: "But alas for you Pharisees, because you pay your tithe of mint and rue and all sorts of garden herbs and neglect justice and the love of God!" (Luke 11:42, NJB; Matthew 23:23). According to Andrews (1958), this word is applied to various kinds of mint. It is the most widely used of all the herbs mentioned in Luke 11 and Matthew 23. In both accounts, Jesus links these herbs with justice.

Many Middle East dishes use large quantities of mint. One of my favorites, called "head of mint" in Arabic, is ground meat mixed with spices and mint, then grilled.

In the Middle East, mint is found growing along watercourses, near springs, and in other wet places. Some species have been introduced to the United States, where they may be minor weed problems in wetlands.

Mint plants in flower in
June, along an irrigation
canal near Ain Auja in
the vicinity of Jericho.

Mulberry

Mulberry: for silkworms and elephants?

THE CLOTHING OF COMMON PEOPLE in the ancient Middle East was linen (flax fiber) or wool, though silk may well have been available for the wealthy from the trading routes of the Far East; the fabled Silk Road terminated in Damascus. Production of silk, which requires the culture of silkworms on mulberry leaves, was likely practiced at the time when the Bible and the Quran were written, though silk production is mentioned in neither book. Silkworm production was widespread in Lebanon and Syria as recently as the early 1900s, the quality of the silk lending its name to "damask" after Damascus.

Silk is explicitly cited in the list of luxury items associated with Babylon: "She [Babylon] bought great quantities of gold, silver, jewels, and pearls; fine linen, purple silk, and scarlet cloth; things made of fragrant thyine wood, ivory goods, and objects made of expensive wood; and bronze, iron, and marble" (Revelation 18:12, NLT). The Greek word used here, *serikos*, is the accepted word for silk.

The mention of silk in the Old Testament is more tenuous. Some scholars translate as silk the word in Proverbs 31:22 that refers to the clothing of the "Woman of Virtue," as well as in a passage in the story of the castaway woman rescued by Jehovah: "I clothed thee also with broidered work, and shod thee with badger's skin, and I girded thee about with fine linen, and I covered thee with silk" (Ezekiel 16:10, KJV). But it is not clear whether silk was readily available at the time the accounts in Proverbs and Ezekiel were written.

Mulberry has become a weedy tree in many places where it was introduced.

Fruit vendor selling mulberry juice (the black fruit in the white pan and in bottles with white caps), in March, in the Hamadiyah Market in Damascus.

The relationship between mulberry and silk is well known: the larvae eat the mulberry leaves. But the connection between elephants and mulberry juice? The Hebrew word translated "mulberry" in the following biblical passage is *tut*, the same word used in present-day Arabic for "mulberry": "The elephants were given a syrup of grapes and mulberries to prepare them for the battle" (I Maccabees 6:34, NJB). Why this particular blend was made for the pachyderms is unclear, though the grape syrup and mulberry juice would be high in energy-yielding calories. The references to silk and mulberry juice seem incontrovertible.

Mulberry is used erroneously in several places in Bible translations. One example is the following passage: "He [Jesus] replied, 'If you have faith as small as a mustard seed, you can say to this mulberry [*sukaminos*] tree, "Be uprooted and planted in the sea," and it will obey you' " (Luke 17:6, NIV). The verse is best understood by knowing that the "mulberry" (NLT), or more accurately "sycamine" (KJV) or "sycamore" (MSG), can be a large tree. Since mulberry (*Morus nigra*) can become a large tree though not as large as the true sycamore, it is understandable that European translators might intercalate the well-known mulberry into the text.

There are several species of mulberry, all in the genus *Morus*, which is in the same family as the fig. But the mulberry that is native to the Middle East was restricted in its range in ancient times. Because of the silk industry and because of the popularity of a drink made from mulberry, the trees are now common throughout suitable habitats in Israel, Lebanon, Jordan, and Syria. The best species for raising silkworms is *Morus nigra*, though other species can be used. The tree has attractive shiny leaves and produces tiny, greenish flowers, from which the characteristic berry-like fruits emerge. For silkworm culture, the tree is coppiced—cut back and allowed to sprout again so the young shoots can be collected for food. The wood is hard and valued for cabinetry (Meiggs 1982).

Mustard

Eruca vesicaria **subspecies** *sativa*, **wild arugula, in March, in Jebel Abdel Aziz, northern Mesopotamia, Syria. Large areas of the** *badia* **(steppe) are covered with masses of white flowers of arugula in the spring.**

MUSTARD IS A WELL-KNOWN condiment. The first thing most Americans envision regarding mustard is a container of the yellow sauce essential with hot dogs. At the same time, mustard is one of the best-known plants in the Bible and the Quran, where it is a symbol of something tiny. Further, in the New Testament, mustard also represents something tiny that can become a monstrous growth.

The Quran offers similar imagery, that of a mustard seed as a measure of the diminutive: "We shall fix the scales of justice on the Day of Resurrection, so that none will be wronged in the least; and even if it were equal to a mustard seed in weight, We shall take it (into account)" (Sura 21:47, Ali); and, "My son, God will bring all things to light, be they as small as a grain of mustard seed, be they hidden inside a rock or in the heavens or the earth" (Sura 31:16, Dawood).

Through parables, Jesus presented profound truths easily understood by ordinary people. He used relevant illustrations from everyday life, so his audience was able to identify with his stories. The mustard plant is an example: "He put another parable before them, 'The kingdom of Heaven is like a mustard seed which a man took and sowed in his field. It is the smallest of all the seeds, but when it has grown it is the biggest of shrubs and becomes a tree, so that the birds of the air can come and shelter in its branches' " (Matthew 13:32, NJB; Mark 4:31; Luke 13:19). It was clear to Jesus's audience what he meant. They had asked questions about the parable of the tares but not the mustard seed. The three features of the mustard plant emphasized by Jesus are the small size of the seed, the large size of the plant in relation to the seed, and the plant's implied rapid growth.

The Greek word for mustard is *sinapi*, uniformly translated as mustard in Matthew 13:31; 17:20; Mark 4:31; Luke 13:19; and Luke 17:6. Candidates are black mustard (*Brassica nigra*), white mustard (*Sinapis arvensis* or *S. alba*), and possibly *S. juncea*. All four plants belong to the mustard family. The leaves are edible, and I have eaten *S. juncea* collected from fields in northern Jordan. After cooking, the taste is pleasant and the pungency reduced. All four plants have small seeds and are characterized by rapid germination and seedling growth, annual habit, and spring flowering. Commercial mustard familiar in Western countries is prepared by grinding the seeds of black and white mustard and mixing them together—a practice unknown to this day in Bible lands.

The Hebrew equivalent is *chardal* (and the modern Arabic cognate is *khardal*), though that word is not included in the Jewish scriptures. The Jewish tradition, however, states that *chardal* is not a garden vegetable, but that it is grown in fields. *Salvadora persica* is one candidate, since Arabs call this plant *khardal* (Post 1901b), but there are strong arguments against this. First, *S. persica* is a desert shrub. Second, it is not cultivated for food or forage, although I have seen camels grazing it. Third, it has a restricted distribution in the Holy Land, being found only in deserts near the Dead Sea. Fourth, the fruits are large and would hardly fit the picture of being among the "smallest of all seeds." In fact, the fruits of *S. persica* are larger than anything usually planted in a garden. Moldenke and Moldenke (1952) provide a helpful summary of reasons why *S. persica* cannot be considered *sinapi*. Therefore, the best candidates for mustard are herbaceous members of the mustard family, Brassicaceae (also known as Cruciferae).

Determining the identity of biblical mustard requires consideration of the literary style of the parables. They are filled with Semitic hyperbole. Mustard plants do not become trees, though I have seen *Sinapis juncea* 3 meters (9 feet) tall near the Hula Swamp in northern Israel. But birds could not lodge in them. In Matthew 13, the emphasis is on small things that become unusually large. This theme pervades all the parables: a sower sows a small seed, the enemy introduces tiny germs of evil, a minute lump of leaven permeates the whole loaf, an invisible treasure turns out to be the real value of a piece of ground, one very precious pearl is worth more than all the possessions of a merchant, an invisible net is drawn through the depths of the sea, and a scribe discovers things hitherto unseen in his treasure. Things that seem small, inconspicuous, hardly worth observation, invisible, turn out to be by far the greatest things.

In addition to the arborescent growth of a garden vegetable, the other image Jesus uses is of a small seed with great potential: "The apostles said to the Lord, 'Increase our faith.' The Lord replied, 'If you had faith like a mustard seed you could say to this mulberry tree, "be uprooted and planted in the sea," and it would obey you'" (Luke 17:5–6, NJB). In addition to the size differential, the other feature of the mustard seed—whether it is *Brassica*, *Sinapis*, or *Eruca*—is rapid germination. Seeds of all three of these genera can begin germination within a few hours after being planted. While this interpretation has not previously been made in the literature, I wonder whether this germination behavior is a reason why Jesus refers to the mustard seed.

For reasons inexplicable, arugula, also known as rocket (*Eruca sativa*, also known as *E. vesicaria* subspecies *sativa*), has not been posited as the mustard of the Bible. It is native to the region and widely cultivated. In the United States, arugula has become increasingly popular in salad mixes. It is easy to grow in a variety of soils and climatic conditions. Seeds are smaller than *Brassica*. Germination is rapid and after a few

Sinapis species in May,
at mouth of Nahr al
Kalb, north of Beirut.

months, the plants reach a height of 1 meter (3 feet). I do not consider this relatively small size a difficulty in exegesis.

Zohary (1982) suggests that wild *Eruca* was the "herbs" sought by Elisha's disciples near Gilgal, which is in the Jordan Valley (II Kings 4:38–39). My observations support this interpretation, because I have collected colycinth fruits in early March, when the fields around Gilgal were covered with *Eruca*. In many parts of steppe regions in the Middle East, *Eruca* produces spectacular displays of white flowers in early spring.

There is meager evidence from Assyria that ancients used both true mustard as well as arugula, at least medicinally. In a formulation for "affection for the temples," a mixture including seed of arugula, sumac, dung from a swallow, pine resin, and roses is fried in a copper pan, kneaded with yeast, and then applied to the temple (Thompson 1937).

The fact that *khardal* is in the Quran is further support that *Eruca* could be interpreted as "mustard." Both *Salvadora* and arugula can grow in arid regions and would be known to residents of Arabia.

Palestinian farmers have told me that the vegetative portions of wild relatives of mustard are collected in the early spring and relished as a cooked vegetable. I have observed the same in Jordan. This use has been documented for *Sinapis* in Turkey (Ertug 1998). Perhaps the leaves were used as a vegetable like many members of the mustard family, a family including such well-known plants as cabbage, turnips, and broccoli.

Mustard seed is an enduring symbol of something small with great potential. Despite its familiarity in modern times, the true identity of the plant referred to in the Bible and the Quran is not certain.

Myrrh

Myrrh purchased in the old market in Damascus.

WHILE MYRRH IS MENTIONED in several places in the Bible (and none in the Quran), the best-known reference is when the magi from the East presented gifts to the Christ child: "When they saw the star, they were filled with joy! They entered the house and saw the child with his mother, Mary, and they bowed down and worshipped him. Then they opened their treasure chests and gave him gifts of gold, frankincense, and myrrh" (Matthew 2:10–11, NLT).

Myrrh is the dried resin of several species of *Commiphora* (Burseraceae). These plants are shrubs or small trees of the arid and semiarid regions of East Africa, Arabia, and the Indian subcontinent. Incisions in the bark allow the resin to exude. When the resin is dry, it is collected and sold. All species are not used for the same purpose: some are used medicinally (Leung and Foster 1996) and others are valued for their fragrance (Calkin and Jellinek 1992). Recent work indicates that *C. myrrha* has opiate qualities (Dolara et al. 1996). This feature helps to interpret a New Testament reference: "And they tried to give Him wine mixed with myrrh; but He did not take it" (Mark 15:23, NASB).

The two different myrrhs, medicinal and fragrant, are both translated from the same Hebrew word, *mor*. The scented myrrh is probably *Commiphora guidottii* (Thulin and Claeson 1991). Odor of myrrh permeates the pages of Solomon's writings, with more references by him than any other Bible author. Song of Solomon has seven references.

Myrrh, *Commiphora kataf,*
in October, near Cave of
Omar in southern Ethiopia.

Species of myrrh
are trees or shrubs
with three-part
leaves. *Commiphora
kataf* in October,
near Cave of Omar,
southern Ethiopia
.

Myrrh tree,
Commiphora kataf, in
October, with incision
scars on the bark from
which resin exuded.

In the single reference in Proverbs, the harlot refers to her bed as having been sprinkled with "myrrh, aloes, and cinnamon" (Proverbs 7:17, NIV). Myrrh is used in a similar way in Song of Solomon, as a personal perfume, and is discussed with erotic overtones: "Then I got up to open to my love, myrrh ran off my hands, pure myrrh off my fingers, on to the handle of the bolt" (Song of Solomon 5:5, NJB); and, "His cheeks are beds of spices, banks sweetly scented. His lips are lilies, distilling pure myrrh" (Song of Solomon 5:13, NJB).

There is a guild of plants associated both with the harlot in Proverbs as well as with the lovers in Song of Solomon. These include cassia, aloes, and myrrh. Myrrh is also linked with frankincense in other verses.

Considerable confusion exists among Bible commentaries and dictionaries about the identification of the plant known as balm or balm of Gilead (Hebrew *tesriy* or *tsoriy*) in the Bible. Zohary (1982) and Hepper (1993) consider balm to be a species of *Commiphora*. There is strong historical precedence for this confusion, since Josephus (Whiston n.d.) writes that the Queen of Sheba brought a plant of *Commiphora* when she visited Solomon. However, myrrh was used long before her arrival in Israel, as a component of the sacred anointing oil (Exodus 30). Myrrh may have been produced near Jericho (Patrich and Arubas 1989), and myrrh oil has been found at Ein Gedi.

With a trail of fragrance throughout the Bible, myrrh is cited as one of the most desirable fragrances. Like a few other plant products, it was widely used in the Levant in ancient times but was not grown there. Myrrh is usually more expensive than frankincense. For example, in Ethiopia frankincense sells for 30 birr (approximately US$3.50) per kilogram (2.2 pounds) while myrrh is 60 birr.

Myrtle

Flowers of myrtle.

MYRTLE WAS A POPULAR ENG-lish female name in the early 1900s. I had two aunt Myrtles, and when I was a child I always thought the name was humorous. Not until I acquired firsthand knowledge of this beautiful plant did I appreciate why girls were named after myrtle. Because myrtle is comely and easily cultivated, it is widely planted as an ornamental shrub in Mediterranean climates.

Myrtle, *Myrtus communis*, is an appealing, unassuming shrub. It has evergreen leaves and under optimum conditions grows to a height of about 8 meters (24 feet). Fragrant, small, white flowers are produced in large numbers in the middle of the summer. The fruit is a small, black berry, resembling a blueberry. In some villages in northeast Syria, an apertif is prepared from myrtle fruits. The entire plant contains fragrant oil. Like several other Bible plants, myrtle is the only representative of its family in the Middle East. The eucalyptus, native to Australia and widely planted in the Middle East, is in the same family.

Myrtle is not mentioned in the Bible until the time of the captivity of the Children of Israel. The first reference is in regard to the celebration of the Feast of Tabernacles (known as Succoth): "And they should proclaim this word and spread it throughout their towns and in Jerusalem: 'Go out into the hill country and bring back branches from olive and wild olive trees, and from myrtles, palms and shade trees, to make booths as it is written'" (Nehemiah 8:15, NIV). Interestingly,

These myrtle branches were
purchased in March at the
Damascus market, at the
time of a Muslim holy day.

myrtle is not expressly mentioned in Leviticus 23:33–40, where rituals of the Feast of Tabernacles are explicated.

Myrtle is included in Isaiah: "I will put the cedar in the wilderness, the acacia, and the myrtle, and the olive tree; I will place the juniper in the desert, together with the box tree and the cypress" (Isaiah 41:19, NASB); and, "Instead of the thornbush the cypress will come up; and instead of the nettle the myrtle will come up" (Isaiah 55:13, NASB). These verses refer to the establishment of the people in the land. As an evergreen, fragrant shrub associated with watercourses, the myrtle is a fitting symbol of the recovery and establishment of God's promises. In Zechariah 1:8–11, a man stands in a ravine among myrtle trees, apparently enjoying their humble beauty and fragrance.

No other uses are given for myrtle in the Bible and it is not mentioned in the Quran. It was used in ancient times for production of ink (Worrell 1947) and perfume (Brun 2000). I have also been told that myrtle leaves are added to the still when making the popular Arab liqueur, *aarak*. A modern use is for decorating graves. During Muslim holy days, there are myrtle vendors by the Shiite shrines in Damascus. The branches are purchased for strewing on the graves of loved ones. The same practice is carried out in Lebanon. This may explain why George Post, the eminent botanist and Bible scholar of the 1800s (Musselman 2006), wrote that myrtle leaves were sold in the markets in his day (Post 1901c) without mentioning their use.

Myrtle needs more attention as a Bible reference. It is an attractive plant even when not flowering, and the entire plant is suffused with a pleasant fragrance.

Nard

Dried rhizomes of spikenard, or nard, *Nardostachys jatamansi*, sold as medicine in Peshawar, Pakistan.

THOUGH CITED IN ONLY THREE places in the Bible, spikenard, or nard, *Nardostachys jatamansi*, is one of the better-known perfumed plants of the scriptures. In Solomon's Song, nard is included in a garden of sensuous delight, to which the Lover compares his Beloved: "Your plants are an orchard of pomegranates with choice fruits, with henna and nard, nard and saffron, calamus and cinnamon, with every kind of incense tree, with myrrh and aloes and all the finest spices" (Song of Solomon 4:13–15, NIV).

Better known is the reference in Jesus's life: "Then Mary took about a pint of pure nard, an expensive perfume; she poured it on Jesus's feet and wiped his feet with her hair. And the house was filled with the fragrance of the perfume. But one of his disciples, Judas Iscariot, who was later to betray him, objected, 'Why was not this perfume sold and the money given to the poor? It was worth a year's wages'" (John 12:3–5; Mark 14:3; NIV). The worth of the ointment was great in ancient times. Nard was traded extensively (Miller 1969). And the plant and its products are highly valued today, especially in ayurvedic medicine.

Because of demand for the plant in India and other countries, there is concern over exploitation of this Himalayan species (Larsen 2005). Nard is rhizomatous and the parts used include the rhizome and sometimes the leaves, which means the entire plant is destroyed. The dried rhizome is used for a variety of remedies, and an oil is extracted from it as well.

Nard belongs to a group of plants like frankincense, myrrh, and thyine, which were widely used in the Middle East though not cultivated there.

Herbalist in Peshawar, Pakistan, discussing the benefits of nard, *Nardostachys jatamansi*, which is highly valued throughout the Himalayan region for its putative medicinal value. Courtesy T. Robert Sampson.

Nettle

**Stinging hairs of
Urtica pilulifera.**

UNLIKE MANY BIBLE PLANTS, nettle is common in north temperate regions.

Some translations use the word "nettle" for these Bible verses: "Among the bushes they cry out; under the nettles they are gathered together" (Job 30:7, NASB); "I passed by the field of the sluggard, and by the vineyard of the man lacking senses, and behold, it was completely overgrown with thistles, its surface was covered with nettles, and its stone wall was broken down" (Proverbs 24:30–31, NASB); "Egypt will round them up, Memphis will bury them; nettles will inherit their fields, and thorn-bushes invade their homesteads" (Hosea 9:6b, NJB; NASB translates as "weeds"); and, "Surely Moab will be like Sodom, and the sons of Ammon like Gomorrah—a place possessed by nettles and salt pits, and a perpetual desolation" (Zephaniah 2:9b, NASB). In the verses noted, NIV does not use "nettles." In that translation, therefore, the identity of what is obviously some kind of weed is not certain. What is certain is that nettles were common throughout the Middle East.

The most widespread nettle in the Middle East is *Urtica pilulifera*. Like other nettles, these weeds grow in areas of high nitrogen concentration, so they are most abundant in places where livestock are kept and around habitations, including ruins and archaeological sites. The entire plant is covered with long, highly specialized hairs that

Camels grazing nettles and other plants at Um al Jamal in northern Jordan in December. Nettles, while stinging, are edible and nutritious for animals and humans. They are commonly found around ruins like this once prosperous Byzantine town.

Urtica pilulifera at the best stage for eating. Boiling destroys the stinging hairs.

can puncture the skin. Each hair is really like a miniature hypodermic needle ready to spring into action. At the tip is a lopsided bulb-like structure that is easily broken at a prestressed spot. When even lightly brushed against, the tip falls off, leaving a sharp point that can easily penetrate skin. At the base of the hair is a reservoir of irritant, believed to be chemically similar to that injected in ant stings; the substance is under pressure and escapes through the tip into the victim. The result is a minor dermatitis that will go away in most individuals after 30 minutes or so. The dermatitis, known as urticaria, gives the genus its Latin name *Urtica*; *pilulifera* refers to the ball-shaped fruits in this species. The seeds are edible but small, and are literally a pain to harvest.

Though not widely appreciated today, nettles were valued by ancient cultures throughout the world as a source of food and fiber. It would not be surprising, therefore, that native nettles would be mentioned in the Bible. However, caution is needed in reaching conclusions, since the word translated "nettles" could mean a different armed plant or, very likely, could be a general term for armed plants.

Oak

At one time, acorns were widely utilized for food. In March, near Mayas, Syria.

O
AK IS ONE OF A GROUP OF BIBLE trees that are well known outside western Asia. The prominence and familiarity of oak in Europe could be the reason that some translations use the word "oak" to simply mean large trees.

Two oaks grow widely in the Middle East, *Quercus calliprinos* and *Q. ithaburensis*, though they are not distinguished from each other in the scriptures. Both can be large, long-lived trees with spreading branches. Because of extensive overgrazing and cutting, large oaks are uncommon in the region today. With their size, longevity, and beauty, it is easy to see why oaks are objects of veneration throughout the world.

As with other large trees, both the oak and the cedar can be a symbol of a mighty man. Several such references are made in the Bible: "Yet it was I who destroyed the Amorite before them, he was as tall as the cedars, as strong as the oaks" (Amos 2:9a, NJB).

Ancient oaks were used for purposes other than timber, including nutrition. The acorns of *Quercus calliprinos* and *Q. ithaburensis*, the oaks that are common in the Levant, are edible, although some trees pro-

"Wail, oaks of Bashan; the dense forest has been cut down!" (Zechariah 11:2b). The oaks of this region have less to wail about since the establishment of an oak preserve near Suweida, Syria. This oak is *Quercus calliprinos*. The grass in the foreground is a wild barley, *Hordeum bulbosum*.

duce extremely bitter acorns. In some regions, acorns were an important food source because of their high starch content and storability. As recently as 2002, I saw acorns sold by a street vendor in Damascus.

Only a fraction of the original oak forests in the Middle East remain because of cutting and overgrazing. The most recent insult was the use of oak for fuel for Ottoman locomotives to maintain the essential Hejaz Railway at the time of the First World War, which decimated the oaks of Bashan.

At one time, the Hauran region, including part of southeastern Syria, was famous for its oaks, the oaks of Bashan mentioned in the Bible: "From oaks of Bashan they made your oars" (Ezekiel 27:6a, NJB). In the early eleventh century, an Arab traveler by the name of Mukaddasi visited the Hauran region and wrote that the natives subsisted on acorns that they ground and mixed with "desert barley" (which I take to be *Hordeum spontaneum*) (le Strange 1896). This report indicates that oaks were abundant in the Hauran at one time, and that the oaks of Bashan are less abundant than in previous centuries.

Oak makes excellent charcoal. Even though the forest preserves in Jordan prohibit cutting and burning of trees, I have seen "charcoal poaching" near the Zubia Preserve in Jordan, indicating the continuing value of this wood for fuel.

Large, open-grown *Quercus ithaburensis* in degraded forest near Ajlon, Jordan. Because of the paucity of wood for building and fuel in the Middle East, most of the large trees there were felled long ago.

Olive

Mature olives in October, Kufur Sumei, Israel.

VENERABLE, UTILITARIAN, AND an integral part of Middle East culture, olive, *Olea europaea*, still plays a role in today's rural society that is similar to its importance in ancient times. The olive tree is native to the Mediterranean region, but most of its relatives are currently found in Africa (Zohary and Hopf 2000).

The olive is considered a divine provision in both the Quran and the Bible: "Let man reflect on the food he eats: how We pour down the rain in torrents and cleave the earth asunder; how We bring forth the corn, the grapes and the fresh vegetation; the olive and the palm, the thickets, the fruit-trees and the green pasture, for you and for your cattle to delight in" (Sura 80:24–32, Dawood; referred to similarly in Deuteronomy 8:8). The Quran has three references to olive.

The Bible has about 25 references to the olive tree and more than 160 references to the oil of the olive. Olive oil had five main uses in Bible days: food, illumination, ointment, soap, and leather and metal preservative. It is safe to assume that any oil mentioned in the Bible is olive oil. Interestingly, there is no record in the Bible of olives being eaten, although that does not mean they were not a food item. On the other hand, the Quran records olives as a condiment: "And a tree that grows out of Mount Sinai which produces oil and a condiment for those who eat" (Sura 23:20, Dawood; Ali translates as "seasoning" rather than condiment).

Well-formed, solitary olive tree in the dry season near the village of Kufur Sumei, northern Galilee, Israel

Olive flowers in May, showing the characteristic four petals and two stamens. Masses of olive flowers have a pleasant though weak fragrance. Antakya (biblical Antioch), Turkey.

The concept of a holy olive tree that provides illumination for God's servants is included in both sacred books. Zerubbabel is told that the oil-producing trees are the anointed of the Lord. An angel said "Also two olive trees by it [a lamp stand], one on the right side of the bowl and the other on its left," and to Zerubbabel's question "What are these, my lord?" the angel answered, "Do you not know what these are? . . . This is the word of the Lord to Zerubbabel saying, 'Not by might nor by power, but by my Spirit' " (Zechariah 4:3–6, NASB).

In the Quran, we read of a blessed olive tree that produces oil that gives light to mankind: "God is the light of the heavens and the earth. The semblance of His light is that of a niche in which is a lamp, the flame within a glass, the glass a glittering star as it were, lit with the oil of a blessed tree, the olive, neither of the East nor of the West, whose oil appears to light up even though fire touches it not—light upon light. God guides to His light whom He will. So does God advance precepts of wisdom for men, for God has knowledge of every thing" (Sura 24:35, Ali). Both of these references show the role that olive oil had in illumination in ancient times.

Oil was a daily commodity for the people of the holy books, and this importance is reflected in several verses. Disobedience to God would result in a loss of the olive crop: "You shall have olive trees throughout your territory but you shall not anoint yourself with the oil, for your olives shall drop off" (Deuteronomy 28:40, NASB). In the wonderful botany lecture on Mount Gerazim where a disgruntled politician, Jotham, likens men to trees, we are reminded of the value of the olive tree: "But the olive tree answered, 'Should I give up my oil, by which both gods and men are honoured, to hold sway over the trees?' " (Judges 9:9, NIV). Olive oil was a component of the anointing oil of the high priest (Exodus 30:24).

Large supplies of olive oil were a sign of prosperity. Excess oil can be stored for up to six years, and such stores were of national concern. For example, in the days of King David, Joash was given the important charge of oil supplies (I Chronicles 27:28b). In addition to lighting, olive oil was used as an ointment for the skin, important in an arid climate: "He [God] makes grass grow for the cattle, and plants for man to cultivate—bringing forth food from the earth; wine that gladdens the heart of man, oil to make his face shine, and bread that sustains his heart" (Psalm 104:14–15, NIV). Lesser known uses were for soap (Jeremiah 2:22; Malachi 3:2) and as a preservative for shields perhaps constructed of wood and overlain with leather as noted in David's lament for Saul: "O mountains of Gilboa, may you have neither dew nor rain, nor fields that yield offerings of grain for there the shield of the mighty was defiled, the shield of Saul—no longer rubbed with oil" (II Samuel 1:21, NIV).

The olive tree is one of the most familiar and characteristic trees in the entire Middle East. Olive oil is prized by Arabs, who use it almost daily. A simple breakfast is just bread and olive oil, the bread often dipped first into a savory mixture of herbs and salt. Large areas are planted in olives; they thrive on the steep and rocky slopes (Deuteronomy 32:13) in carefully maintained terraces.

These venerable trees are attractive: "His [the restored Israel] branches shall spread, and his beauty shall be as the olive tree, and his smell as Lebanon" (Hosea 14:6, KJV); and, "Thy wife shall be as a fruitful vine by the sides of thine house: thy children like olive plants round about thy table" (Psalm 128:3, KJV). In the dry season, the olive tree, with its refreshing green leaves, presents a distinctive contrast against the dry, brown hills. Leaves are evergreen, dark graygreen above and gray beneath. With a slight breeze, the trees appear silver, and in the dry season the wind makes the hillsides glisten. The undersurface of the leaf is covered with microscopic, overlapping scales.

The remarkable root system of the olive tree is the secret of its survival in its dry, rocky habitat. To produce a good crop, however, the trees need care throughout the year—careful pruning, cultivating, and fertilizing. The olive tree produces sprouts at its base. Today, olives are often grown on grafted stock; a rapidly growing rootstock is selected and a good-quality scion is put in it. But in Bible days, olives were often grown directly from the sprouts. The olive farmer would select sprouts from his best trees, carefully remove them, and plant them where they would be tended. Psalm 128:3 may be a reference to this practice: "Your sons will be like olive shoots round your table."

The olive tree does not become very tall and lives for up to 1000 years, producing fruit throughout its long life. Trunks often become gnarled, bent, and hollow inside, yet the tree continues to produce fruit. Because of this growth pattern, the wood is unsuitable for building, but it is hard, with an attractive grain, so it is used today for the manufacture of small items.

Olive wood is mentioned only in I Kings 6:32 (NIV) for the construction of several articles in the temple, especially a door. It would be difficult to find a piece of olive wood large enough to make a door. The I Kings reference could be to sandalwood (*Santalum album*), which is not native to Israel but imported from India. Possibly the doors were made from a composite of many small pieces of olive. The identity of this wood remains unknown.

About the first of May, the olive begins to flower. The flowers are white, small, and only slightly scented. They come and go scarcely without notice, largely obscured by the evergreen leaves. Olive is from a family of plants well known for fragrance, including lilac and jasmine, and therefore it is a modest member of an otherwise showy family.

In the autumn, the olive bears fruit. Olives today are harvested in villages as in Bible times by carefully beating the trees with sticks and then picking up the olives from the ground. This process may appear to damage the olive tree, but as for other trees like walnut, beating the tree for the fruits stimulates additional bud production.

When ripe, the olive is jet black and attractive. If you enjoy olives, you would be tempted to eat one right off the tree, but a fresh olive is bitter and unpalatable. To be used, olives are soaked in brine to remove the bitter component in the aqueous part of the fruit. The olive must be crushed to express the oil. Until recently, in villages olives were crushed between giant stones driven by draft animals, as in ancient times. Today hydraulic presses are used. For oil, the olives are harvested while green. Only a few are allowed to fully mature, and they are used for condiments.

The "wild olive tree" is mentioned in the Bible: "Now suppose that some branches were broken off, and you are wild olive, grafted among the rest to share with the others the rich sap of the olive tree; then it is not for you to consider yourself superior to the other branches; and if you start feeling proud, think: it is not you that sustain the root, but the root that sustains you" (Romans 11:17–18, NJB; a reference in Nehemiah 8:15 is likely not a wild olive.) But the only New Testament reference, in Romans, undoubtedly refers to a wild or at least uncultivated olive. Farmers have referred to trees that spontaneously come up in their olive groves as "wild olives." These trees have a different aspect from the carefully cultivated olives but they probably only represent sports from the larger population. These are the forms Green (2002) refers to as "feral olives"; he designates them as *Olea europaea* var. *sylvestris*.

Onion

Field of onions in May, near Tubas, Palestinian Territories.

Although onion, *ALLIUM CEPA*, today is an essential component of Middle East cuisine, there is a solitary reference to onion in the Bible and none in the Quran. Onions were among the desired foods of Egypt by the dissembling Children of Israel (Numbers 11:5). The origins of the onion are still being debated (Zohary and Hopf 2000), though there are numerous indigenous *Allium* species in the region.

Onion has been a food for millennia, both in Egypt and Mesopotamia (Murray 2000).

Onion is easily grown from seed, and after germination the small seedlings are set out to mature. While the main purpose of onion was obviously as a food, onions have been found inside mummies, indicating a role in the preservation of the body or as an aid to the person in the afterlife.

Field of onions in June, near
Ramallah, Palestinian Territories.
Watchtowers like the one in the
background were once a common
feature in fields of highly valued
crops; a guard would live there
and watch for poachers.

Papyrus

Flowers and fruits of papyrus are tiny and borne in large numbers in globe-shaped masses.

WHILE GIANT CANE AND COMmon reed are the most widespread of Bible wetland plants, perhaps the best known is bulrush mentioned in the story of baby Moses (Exodus 2), where the child was hidden in the vegetation along the Nile River. Still found in parts of the Nile Valley, bulrush, or papyrus (*Cyperus papyrus*), occurs throughout much of Africa. Papyrus is the source of the English word "paper." Paper was made by pounding the soft papyrus stems together, one layer of stems at right angles to the other, to form a sheet.

Papyrus is an obligate aquatic plant. Its distribution in the Middle East and Egypt has been reduced by the draining of wetlands and otherwise altering waterways. The plant grows in large mats, often forming floating islands, at the margins of rivers, in lakes, and along impoundments. Resembling a grass but in a related family, papyrus has a round stem several meters (6 feet or more) tall that bears a spherical mass of tiny flowers on long, flexuous stalks. The thick stems are filled with cells that contain air, which may be the reason why papyrus is called *agam* (with variations), meaning "absorbent" in Hebrew. In some places, for example, papyrus is the translation for *cuwph* (Exodus 2:3, NIV).

The large air spaces in the stout stems provided buoyancy when used in making boats. In Isaiah, an apparent reference is made to the

Mats of papyrus in the Hula
Swamp in northern Israel.
This site is the only one in
the Middle East with extant
papyrus populations, and
now is a preserve. In the early
1900s, there was a big industry
for baskets, mats, and other
items made from papyrus.

Nile: "Woe to the land of whirring wings [or locusts] along the rivers of Cush [the region of southern Egypt and adjacent Sudan and Ethiopia], which sends envoys by sea in papyrus boats over the water" (Isaiah 18:1–2, NIV).

At one time, there was a large population of papyrus in northern Israel in an area that the Bible refers to as the waters of Merom (Joshua 11:5) or Lake Merom. This swamp, the Hula Swamp, was a malarial area. So Zionists drained most of it in the early 1900s, destroying the habitat of the papyrus, the northernmost population of this plant in the world. Fortunately, there has been a concerted effort to restore part of the Hula Swamp, and it is now possible to visit the area and see impressive stands of papyrus.

Paper as a writing material is mentioned in only one place in the Bible. In Isaiah 19:7, the Hebrew word *arah* is translated "paper reed" in the KJV, perhaps an illusion to papyrus. The NIV renders this as "plants along the Nile," which could also be papyrus. The only New Testament reference is: "I have much to write to you, but I do not want to use paper and ink" (II John 12a, NIV). *Chartes*, the Greek word used here, is related to the English word "chart." Greeks imported papyrus via the Phoenician town of Byblos, from which comes our word "bible" and related terms. Thus, in New Testament times, paper was well known to writers such as the Apostle John.

Despite the enormous impact of the papyrus plant on the development of writing and books, it is almost extirpated in the Middle East.

Pine

EVERYONE KNOWS THE GENERAL architecture of a pine tree, that it has cones, and that the sap of the tree is resinous and sticky. Because of this familiarity, some of the trees in the Bible may have been translated erroneously as pine; it remains unclear whether these gymnosperm trees were intended in the text.

Three pines are frequently encountered in the Middle East: stone pine, Aleppo pine (after Aleppo, Syria), and Calabrian (after Italy's Calabria region) pine. *Pinus pinea*, the stone pine (so-called because of its hard seeds), also known as umbrella pine (an allusion to its umbrella-like appearance when mature), is grown for its seeds (pine nuts), an important ingredient in Middle East foods. (Pinyon nuts are also pine seeds, but from a native North American pine.) Today, most of these seeds are imported from China and may be produced by trees other than the stone pine. And there is evidence that cultivation of stone pine, a Mediterranean species, was not widespread in ancient times (Biger and Liphschitz 1991).

Serotinous cones of Aleppo pine (*Pinus halepensis*) in March, planted as part of a restoration effort at the Jebel Abdel Aziz Preserve, northern Mesopotamia, Syria. The reflexed cones borne on stalks are characteristic of this species.

The two native pines are Aleppo pine, *Pinus halepensis* (ironically apparently not native to Aleppo), and Calabrian pine, *P. brutia*. Some forests of Aleppo pine remain in Israel and Jordan. Biger and Liphschitz (1991) suggest that *P. brutia* was absent from what is modern-

day Israel, being more common farther north. Calabrian pine is wide-spread in Syria and Turkey. Liphschitz and Biger (2001) present convincing evidence that Aleppo pine also was not formerly widespread in what is modern-day Israel and Jordan.

The two species *Pinus halepensis* and *P. brutia* are quite similar, so I have difficulty distinguishing them. They are immediately recognizable as pines because of the typical architecture of branches and the leaves (needles) that pines have. Despite their similarity, there is convincing evidence that they represent two distinct species (Madmon et al. 2003). Both pines belong to a guild of plants associated with fire-maintained communities.

Among their adaptations to fire are persistent lower branches that can carry flame to the crowns of the trees, where the cones will open in response to heat. Both of these pines have serotinous cones: retention of mature seeds in cones in a canopy-stored seed bank that ensures delayed dispersal (Ne'eman et al. 2004). In general, pines that have nonpruning branches do not produce the most desirable timber because of the presence of knots that weaken the ability of the wood to carry weight. Therefore, it is unlikely that pine was used in the ancient Middle East in the same way as, for example, cedar or open-grown (in contrast to fastigate) cypress, which have long boles (the distance from the ground to the first branch).

In light of these considerations, is pine mentioned anywhere in the Bible? I do not think it is possible to say with certainty that any verses explicitly refer to pine. However, there is one pine product that is often overlooked in the context of the Bible. That is pitch, the material extracted from pine trees for caulking ships and sealing wine amphoras. Both *Pinus halepensis* and *P. brutia* are recorded as producing pitch and turpentine in the ancient Mediterranean (Meiggs 1982), though

Aleppo pine, *Pinus halepensis,* in April, on a ridge above the Jizreel Valley. This pine has persistent lower branches, indicative of a tree adapted to fire ecology.

Forest of Aleppo pine near Dibbeen, Jordan. Fire plays an important role in the reproduction of this species as with many pines.

Cones of pine, likely *Pinus brutia*, carved on Roman ruins at Palmyra, Syria. The inclusion of this pine in this relief suggests that the plant was well known and valued.

these materials are lacking in Egyptian archaeology (Serpico 2000). It could be that the pitch used in constructing Noah's ark was derived from pine: "So make yourself an ark of cypress wood; make rooms in it and coat it with pitch inside and out" (Genesis 6:14, NIV). The basket into which baby Moses was placed was coated with pitch, likely derived from pine, as well as bitumen: "But when she could hide him no longer, she got a papyrus basket for him and coated it with tar and pitch. Then she placed the child in it and put it among the reeds along the bank of the Nile" (Exodus 2:3, NIV). An entirely different use is reported by Levey (1954): that resin from gymnosperms was used in the Assyrian empire for the production of soap.

Whether pine can be documented in the Bible or not, the tree is an important and conspicuous element of the landscape in areas of the Levant with higher rainfall.

Pistachio

Fresh pistachios sold by street vendors in Amman, Jordan.

NATIVE TO THE NEAR EAST AND southwest Asia (Zohary and Hopf 2000), pistachio trees (*Pistacia vera*) are widely cultivated in the Middle East. It is not surprising that Jacob would include them as a special treat from Canaan to present to the leader of Egypt: "Then their father Israel said to them, 'If it must be, then do this: Put some of the best products of the land in your bags and take them down to the man as a gift—a little balm and a little honey, some spices and myrrh, some pistachio nuts and almonds'" (Genesis 43:11, NIV). Aleppo, Syria, is famous for the production of pistachios, which are known in Arabic as "nuts of Aleppo."

Pistachio is in the same family as poison ivy, as well as mangos and cashews. For this reason, people who are sensitive to poison ivy are often adversely affected by eating raw pistachios.

Like the flowers of its relatives, flowers of pistachio are green and inconspicuous. The trees can be quite large. They have dark green, compound leaves. Pistachio flowers in the spring and, because the trees are unisexual, only one male tree is planted among female trees. In the late summer, the fruits develop. Technically these fruits are drupes, with a fleshy outer part covering the seed. The outer part is red, and that is why pistachio shells are sometimes dyed red. In the Middle East, the young fruits are eaten. After the fleshy part of the fruit is removed, the seeds are allowed to dry and crack, revealing the seed, or pistachio nut.

Developing pistachios in an
orchard near Aleppo, Syria.

Plane

Developing fruit of
Platanus orientalis
near Ajlon, Jordan

THE ORIENTAL PLANE TREE, *PLAT-anus orientalis*, is a close relative of the common sycamore, *Platanus occiden-talis*, of eastern North America. It is a putative parent of the London plane tree widely planted in north temperate regions and usually considered a hybrid between *P. orientalis* and *P. occidentalis* (*P. ×hispanica* 'Acerifolia'). In several translations of the Bible, a species of fig is called "sycamore," a corruption of "sycamine" and not the plane tree.

The oriental plane tree has broad leaves, mottled brown and white bark, and small, inconspicuous flowers that develop into spherical ball-like fruits. A first encounter with a plane tree draws attention to the unusual bark: the white and brown patches remind me of the markings on a giraffe. The young branches of the tree are white; the trunks of older trees are dark brown. The plane tree frequently sloughs patches of bark, which enables it to survive in areas with serious air pollution: toxic materials are sequestered in the bark that the tree handily sheds.

The largest native stands of this tree I have observed are along the upper reaches of the Jordan River in Israel and also along the Litani and Dog Rivers (Nahr al Kalb) in Lebanon. But sizable specimens are also found near springs. Although the tree may reach a good size, the wood is not as desirable as oak or pistacio; it is difficult to work because of its characteristic cross-fibers. It is now commonly planted as a shade tree along streets of the region.

Plane tree in March,
Barada River, Damascus.

The mottled bark is
characteristic of the
plane tree. In March,
in Damascus, along
the Barada River.

While the oriental plane tree was widely planted in Greek and Roman periods and linked with Socrates and Pliny (Meiggs 1982), it is less certain that this tree can be included in a definitive list of trees of the holy books. It is not included in the Quran, and its possible exclusion from the biblical text may be a result of its inferior wood or because of its limited distribution, usually near perennial rivers or springs.

Two likely places where plane is suggested are verses in Genesis and Ezekiel. In what might be the first case of genetic engineering in history, Jacob designed an experiment to insure that he would indeed receive the blessing promised to him by God. His hypothesis was simple—if the goats saw mottled branches while they were in heat, the product of fertilization would lead to mottled goats, and he told Laban he would segregate these livestock from Laban's holdings as his payment: "Jacob then got fresh shoots from poplar [*Populus euphratica*], almond [*Prunus dulcis*] and plane trees, and peeled them in white strips, laying bare the white part of the shoots. He set up the shoots he had peeled in front of the animals, in the troughs, in the waterholes where the animals came to drink. Since they mated when they came to drink, the goats thus mated in front of the shoots and so the goats produced striped, spotted and speckled young" (Genesis 30:37–39, NJB). I consider that plane tree fits well here because poplar is found along watercourses, though almond is not a wetland tree.

In Ezekiel, the King of Egypt is likened to a tree, a simile used elsewhere in the Quran and the Bible regarding people: "There was no cedar like it in the garden of God, no cypress had branches such as these, no plane tree could match its boughs, no tree in the garden of God could rival its beauty" (Ezekiel 31:8, NJB). Because a feature of the oriental plane is its large boughs, the image of that tree fits in this verse, though caution is needed in being too literal about an image.

Pomegranate

Pomegranate fruit, with its distinctive persistent calyx, in Cana, Galilee, Israel.

POMEGRANATE, *PUNICA GRANATUM,* is one of the provisions of Allah: "It is He who sends down water from the sky with which We bring forth the buds of every plant. From these We bring forth green foliage and close-growing grain, palm-trees lade with clusters of dates, vineyards and olive groves, and pomegranates alike and different. Behold their fruits when they ripen. Surely in these there are signs for true believers" (Sura 6:99, Dawood). There are three references to this widely grown fruit in the Quran.

Pomegranate is referred to 17 times in the Bible. Of the "six species of the land" in Deuteronomy 8:8, pomegranate is certainly the most beautiful. In addition to fruit production, the shrub is planted in many parts of the world as an ornamental, and dwarf varieties with large flowers have become popular with gardeners. When grown for its fruit, pomegranate has many stems arising from the base, with small, dark leaves; it can reach a height of about 3 meters (about 9 feet). Pomegranate trees requires little care compared to other fruit trees, so they are often planted in marginal areas where they still produce fruit.

The flowers, produced in the spring, are strikingly beautiful, with a bright red-orange color and delicate bell shape. They are used in folk medicines, including for childbirth, perhaps because the flower shape has a fanciful resemblance to the uterus.

Pomegranate fruits in
July, near Ajlon, Jordan.

The fruits begin to mature in the first half of August. They are large, up to 15 centimeters (6 inches) across. As noted in the Quran verse, there are many varieties of pomegranates. Some are sweet and eaten as a dessert. Others are tart and are used either as a substitute for lemon in cooking or to make a refreshing drink. Each fruit contains hundreds of hard, small seeds. Unlike most seeds, which have a seed coat that is hard and durable, like bean, the outer seed coat of the pomegranate is fleshy and is the source of the juice that makes the fruit desirable. The unique, fleshy seed coat in pomegranate, known technically as a sarcotesta, is widely used in the Middle East to prepare a pleasantly sour drink, as referred to in Song of Solomon: "I would give you spiced wine to drink, the nectar of my pomegranates" (Song of Solomon 8:2b, NIV). The juice contains as much as 17 milligrams per kilogram of oestrone, a compound being investigated for advantageous properties in cancer research (Fernandes-Carlos et al. 1997).

The tough, leathery rind of the pomegranate fruit is crimson and other colors of red. Because of the rind's high tannin content, it has been used to tan leather. And the red flesh is sometimes used to dye cloth and carpets.

Pomegranate imagery is prominent in two places in the Bible: the garment of the high priest and in the temple. Bells and pomegranates alternate on the skirt of the high priest: "And on the skirts thereof thou shalt make pomegranates of blue, and purple, and scarlet, round about the skirts thereof; and bells of gold between them round about" (Exodus 28:33, KJV). Engraved on the capitals of the two pillars at the front of Solomon's temple were 200 pomegranates. Above the pomegranates were lilies. When the Children of Israel were taken into captivity, the pomegranates on the pillars are specifically mentioned (Jeremiah 52:22–23).

The Song of Solomon contains several references to pomegranates, no doubt because of the symmetry and beauty of the fruit: "Your temples behind your veil are like the halves of a pomegranate" (Song of Songs 4:3a; 6:7; NIV); "Your plants are an orchard of pomegranates with choice fruits" (4:13a, NIV); "I went down to the grove of nut trees to look at the new growth in the valley, to see if the vines had budded or the pomegranates were in bloom" (6:11, NIV); and, "Let us go early to the vineyards to see if the vines have budded, if their blossoms have opened, and if the pomegranates are in bloom—there I will give you my love" (7:12, NIV).

Poplar

Closeup of Euphrates poplar male flowers in March, Deir Ezzor, Syria.

TWO DIFFERENT POPLARS ARE MEN-tioned in the scriptures: the white poplar (*Populus alba*) and the Euphrates poplar (*Populus euphratica*). White poplar is familiar in North America and Europe because it is often planted as a rapidly growing shade tree. The younger portions of the stem are usually a bright white; leaves are covered with dense hairs beneath, but the upper surface is dark green. In the Middle East, the white poplar is often common along rivers and is frequent near the Banias Spring, one of the sources of the Jordan; it is also widely planted. White poplar has been introduced to North America and is commonly planted, though the wood is brittle and the tree is short lived.

This tree may be the one referred to in the genetics experiment of Jacob: "Then Jacob took some fresh branches from poplar, almond, and plane trees and peeled off strips of bark, making white streaks on them. Then he placed these peeled branches in the watering troughs where the flocks came to drink, for that was where they mated. And when they mated in front of the white-streaked branches, they gave birth to young that were streaked, speckled, and spotted. Jacob separated those lambs from Laban's flock. And at mating time he turned the flock to face Laban's animals that were streaked or black. This is how he built his own flock instead of increasing Laban's" (Genesis 30:37–40, NLT).

Grove of white poplar, *Populus alba*, at Banias, northern Israel.

Male flowers on a large Euphrates poplar (*Populus euphratica*) tree in March, on the Euphrates River, Deir Ezzor, Syria. Like other poplars, Euphrates poplar has distinctive hanging masses of unisexual flowers in the early spring.

The second poplar is the Euphrates poplar, *Populus euphratica*, which forms a conspicuous part of the vegetation of the lower Jordan River. Along the Euphrates River, *P. euphratica* is also a characteristic tree. Like white poplar and other poplar species, this tree is clonal: underground it grows extensive rhizomes, from which sprout new little trees. Also, you can break off a branch, stick it in the ground, and a tree will grow. Branches that drop from the tree can be carried some distance by the river, and that branch can take root on a far sandbar or bank, forming a new tree.

In common with some other species of poplar, the leaves are polymorphic: different leaves on the same tree or even the same branch may have strikingly different shapes.

The bark of *Populus euphratica*, unlike its close relative the white poplar, is not white, and the leaves do not have a white undersurface. It can tolerate relatively high salinity. Common in many parts of the Middle East, Euphrates poplar is assumed to be intended in Psalm 137:1–3 (KJV), where the captives hung their harps on the "willows" of Babylon (but see NIV, which uses poplar rather than willow). The commonly planted "weeping willow" was given its name, *Salix babylonica*, after this portion of scripture. However, it is native to China and did not grow in Bible lands. Like so many other Bible plants, the wording used to describe poplars as "willows" in the King James Version leads to a misrepresentation of the text. While the image of hanging the harps is figurative, the thin branches of willows would not support harps.

Reed

Jordan River with reed, *Phragmites australis*, on both banks. With strong, extensive rhizomes, this woody grass transgresses one of the most volatile international borders with impunity.

COMMON REED, *PHRAGMITES AUSTRALIS*, like cane, is a member of the grass family, though it is characteristically found in wetter sites than cane. It is unusual in growing throughout most of the world. For example, extensive stands occur in the delta of the Danube River near the Black Sea. In North America, the same species has developed especially aggressive races that are destroying some natural wetlands. Common reed is also frequent throughout the Middle East. Reaching a height of 4 meters (12 feet), it is a hardy plant of marshes, with tough, aggressive rhizomes.

The Bible offers graphic descriptions of battles in Babylon, a city near rivers with marshes: "One courier follows another and messenger follows messenger to announce to the king of Babylon that his entire city is captured,

Reeds are cut and dried for fuel. In the foreground is a pile of branches and reed stems. The brown area along the Euphrates is a stand of reed. East of Manbij, Syria, in March.

By the end of summer, the reed stems have hardened and are cut for use in building. In this traditional mud house along the Kharbur River in Syrian Mesopotamia the reed provides support for the mud roof.

the river crossings seized, the marshes set on fire and the soldiers terrified" (Jeremiah 51:31–32, NIV). The Hebrew word "marshes" in the NIV is *agam*. Babylon's marshes may have been dominated by common reed, which forms dense stands along the Tigris and Euphrates Rivers and in oases.

One such oasis is the famed Azraq Oasis in Jordan, which has suffered from reckless draining in recent years. Further damage has been incurred by the removal of water for the city of Amman. The permanent lakes at Azraq made it the largest oasis within thousands of square kilometers of desert. With a lowering of the water table, common reed invaded and today forms the dominant vegetation in the vastly reduced oasis, which, ironically, must be maintained by pumping water into the oasis.

It was a bright, still March day in 1998 when I visited Azraq Oasis with other biologists. Concerned about the overwhelming dominance of *Phragmites* that crowded out other, more desirable species and lowered diversity of plants and animals, we surveyed the area and then left for the Azraq Preserve office on a low hill overlooking the marsh. Suddenly the sky was filled with billows of black smoke from the marsh. The stand of common reed was ablaze. Rushing to the fire, we were held back by the heat and the roar. As the reed burns, water vapor builds up in the stem, and it pops, making a loud sound. I could identify with the soldiers at the margin of the marsh in Jeremiah 51, terrified as the marsh burned out of control!

Although not discussed in the Bible or the Quran, reed had several uses in the Middle East. Like giant cane, *Arundo donax*, the stems could be used to make writing quills. And the leaves and stems were used to weave mats, some of which have survived in Egyptian tombs (Wendrich 2000).

Rose

The attractive, fragrant flowers of this rose shrub, *Rosa phoenicia*, are produced in May. Near the Chouf Cedar Preserve on Mount Lebanon.

A ROSE BY ANY NAME IS, IN THE scriptures, not a rose. Perhaps no other plants in the Bible have been more misrepresented than entries translated "rose." This situation is not surprising since roses were well known in Europe at the time of early Bible translations, and even used as symbols for the Royal Stuarts—England even had a War of the Roses. So it would be natural for these early scholars, removed from the flora of the Middle East, to translate an attractive plant as a rose. The best-known example is the "rose" of Sharon: "I am the rose of Sharon, the lily of the valley" (Song of Solomon 2:1, NIV). Despite uncertainty as to its proper determination, this plant is not a rose. In another verse, "I have grown tall as a palm in Ein-Gedi, as the rose bushes of Jericho" (Ecclesiasticus 24:14, NJB), the placing of the rose in Jericho is ecologically unlikely, since Jericho is an oasis in an arid region, not a place where roses are likely to be found—though they could be in a garden. Moldenke and Moldenke (1952) provide an excellent overview of some of the different ways "rose" has been translated.

Roses are in the genus *Rosa* and have been cultivated since ancient times. The literature on this economically important genus is vast and the history of rose introductions and breeding is extensive. There are native roses in Bible lands, attractive showy plants that certainly are well known to residents. They are all shrubs, usually well armed, technically not with thorns (which botanists consider modified branches) but with prickles (outgrowths of any plant surface), and with large, attractive flowers. These roses are usually white or light pink in the most widely distributed Levant rose, *Rosa phoenicia*.

Exculpating roses from the biblical text does not demean these well-known showy shrubs but does improve the accuracy of the texts.

Phoenician rose, *Rosa phoenicia*, widespread in the Middle East, has flowers that are light pale pink to darker hues as in this shrub near the Chouf Cedar Preserve on Mount Lebanon, in May.

Rose of Sharon

Rose of Sharon, *Gladiolus italicus,* **in May, on Mount Lebanon at 1000 meters (3281 feet) near the town of Mukhtara.**

EW BIBLE PLANTS ARE BETTER known than the rose of Sharon: "I am a rose of Sharon, a lily of the valleys" (Song of Solomon 2:1, NIV). More accurately, the name of the plant is well known, but the precise identity is uncertain and it is not a rose (genus *Rosa*). The only clue to what is obviously a strongly figurative image is the ecology—the plant is linked with the Plain of Sharon. Sharon is the fertile coastal plain, 60 kilometers (50 miles) long and about 17 kilometers (10 miles) wide that parallels the Mediterranean in the northern half of Israel. The plant associated with this area of intensive agriculture is likely adapted to cultivated fields, not other habitats such as forests or marshes. The "rose of Sharon" must therefore be able to tolerate shallow cultivation, which would have been the norm in Bible days with draught animals and plowing. Several plants can be considered. In addition to *Rosa* species, tulip (*Tulipa* species) and daffodil (*Narcissus* species) have been suggested as "rose of Sharon."

Assuming that the weed flora of modern grain fields (in traditional cultivation, not in large-scale mechanized cultivation) is similar to that of Bible times, I believe that *Gladiolus italicus* and the closely related if not conspecific *G. atroviolaceus* could be the rose of Sharon. I have seen them in fields maintained traditionally, small plots in Palestine, Lebanon, and Syria, planted with grains or legumes and cultivated either

Rose of Sharon, *Gladiolus italicus*, a
relative of the garden gladiolus, graces
fields that are so shallowly plowed
the rootstock is not destroyed.

by hand or with animal power. They thrive under these conditions because they flower at the end of the rainy season before the crop is harvested and the field is left fallow until plowing in the early fall. The plants are probably spread by asexual reproduction from the corm by the disturbance of cultivation. These relatives of the common garden gladiolus resemble their cultivated cousins, with distinct pointed leaves and large, showy flowers.

Rose of Sharon, like the balm of Gilead, is embedded in church language and culture. The fact that neither of these two notables can be identified with precision does not diminish their lore.

Rue

The leaves of rue are used for flavoring, to make teas, and for medicine.

RUE, *RUTA CHALEPENSIS*, IS MENtioned once in the Bible: "Woe to you Pharisees, because you give God a tenth of your mint, rue and all other kinds of garden herbs, but you neglect justice and the love of God. You should have practiced the latter without leaving the former undone" (Luke 11:42, NIV).

Rue is native to the Middle East and is still widely grown, especially by rural people. It is a short-lived, perennial plant and a member of the same family as citrus; like citrus plants, it has a pungent oil throughout. The flowers are bright yellow. Villagers use the leaves as an herbal tea. Once, in a Palestinian village in Galilee, I ate black olives that were preserved in olive oil with rue leaves. The taste was appealing, but ingesting parts of the plant may not be prudent. There have been documented cases of photosensitization caused by light reacting with compounds in the blood stream, resulting in an allergic reaction.

Of the four plants mentioned in Luke as the hypocritical tithes of the Pharisees—mint, dill, cumin, and rue—only rue has a wide range of medical applications (Mansour et al. 1990), and it is only mentioned in Luke's gospel. Could it be that Luke, a physician, was familiar with the plant for its medical use and may even have prescribed it?

In the Levant, rue is called *rehan* in Arabic. However, Farooqi (2001, 2003) links *rehan* with basil, *Ocimum basilicum*.

Rue growing in the wild near
Ajlon, Jordan. This plant is
an infrequent resident in
the maquis vegetation.

Saffron

Saffron blooming in my garden in November in Norfolk, Virginia. The corms were collected in Andalucia, Spain.

SAFFRON IS THE MOST EXPENSIVE spice known. One kilogram (2.20 pounds) costs more than US$1000! About 150 saffron flowers are needed to produce less than 0.05 ounce (14 grams) of spice. The dried stigmata are known as threads, and 75,000 flowers are needed to produce the threads in 1 pound (454 grams) of the final product. Because of its economic importance, there is extensive literature on the culture, medicinal value, and use of saffron (Fernández and Abdullaev 2004; Kafi et al. 2006). Despite the plant's ancient use as a spice, it is only mentioned as an ornamental in the Old Testament.

Saffron, *Crocus sativus*, is a fall-blooming crocus with narrow, grass-like leaves and large, purple flowers that last only one day. The dark red stigmata droop between the corolla lobes, contrasting with the erect, bright-yellow stamens. As with other members of the genus, flowers and leaves are produced from a corm, a bulb-like underground stem. In contrast to most other crocuses, saffron is a sterile triploid (triploids have an unbalanced set of chromosomes that do not allow them to reproduce) so cannot yield seed. Saffron reproduces vigorously by buds from the corm.

This delightfully fragrant flower is referred to only once in the Bible: "Your thighs shelter a paradise of pomegranates with rare spices— henna with nard, nard and saffron, fragrant calamus and cinnamon,

Frequently sold in Middle Easter bazaars under the name *zafran*, this product is actually the dried flowers of safflower, *Carthamus tinctorius*. I purchased this *zafran* in Amman, Jordan.

Crocus flowers ready to be harvested in October, in Andalucia, Spain. The large, drooping, red stigmata are evident. When dried, the dark red threads become the saffron of commerce.

with all the trees of frankincense, myrrh, and aloes, and every other lovely spice" (Song of Solomon 4:13–14, NLT). All plants mentioned in this verse are known for their fragrance, though they all have other uses as well. This collection of sensuous plants suggests that saffron was well known in Solomon's day.

Spain is the largest producer of commercial saffron, mostly from the Andalucia region, where the crop is harvested in October. Plants grow in small plots, less than 0.25 hectare (0.62 acre). Flowers are collected in baskets and taken home, where the threads are removed. Immediately after removal, the stigmata are carefully dried over a cool fire, often charcoal, a process that darkens the color and develops the flavor.

In the spring, corms are planted at a depth of about 2 inches (5 centimeters). Numerous flowers are produced the first year, but the second year is the most productive in terms of flowers. After three years, the corms are dug; the larger corms are discarded and the smaller ones are replanted. In Iran and Kashmir, both important saffron-producing areas, corms are left in the ground for up to 12 years. Due to demand, saffron culture is expanding in such countries as Morocco and Iran.

Visitors to the spice markets in Middle East bazaars have told me what wonderful deals they got on saffron, paying something like US$1 for 1 kilo. The confusion, not entirely undeliberate, comes from applying the Arabic word for saffron, *zafran*, to the dried flowers of safflower, *Carthamus tinctorius*. Safflower is better known as a source of healthy cooking oil than for their dried flowers, which are used to color rice. Safflower has little, if any taste, but does impart a kind of saffron color to food, so it is a common plant in home gardens in several Middle Eastern countries.

Sycomore

Sycomore fruits in May, from Sidon, Lebanon

BIBLE READERS ARE OFTEN SUR-prised that the diminutive tax collec-tor, Zacchaeus, climbed up in a kind of fig tree to be able to see Jesus: "And, behold, there was a man named Zacchaeus, which was the chief among the publicans, and he was rich. And he sought to see Jesus who he was; and could not for the press, because he was little of stature. And he ran before, and climbed up into a sycamore tree to see him: for he was to pass that way" (Luke 19:1–4, KJV). Though this translation is close to the original Greek, there has been confusion about the identity of "sycamore."

That this tree is *Ficus sycomorus* seems unequivocal. The Hebrew is *shawkawm* and the Greek *sukaminos*, similar words for this important tree. The sycamore fig is unrelated to the common sycamore (*Platanus occidentalis*) of the Eastern United States. Likewise, the English syca-more is actually a maple (*Acer pseudoplatanus*). The imputation of Bible plant names into local flora is a common phenomenon, especially since the translators of the influential King James Version had little first-hand knowledge of plants of the Middle East.

Sycamore (the preferred spelling) is a large tree up to 10 meters (30 feet) tall with a spreading crown and large, leathery, alternate leaves. Flowers are minute and borne in specialized structures termed "syconia" (singular "syconium"). Syconia are found only in this genus and represent a highly evolved pollination structure involving min-

Old, protected sycomore tree at Our Lady of Mantara Church, in May, in Sidon, Lebanon. When sycomore fruits mature, local citizenry come to gather them.

Ripe sycomore fruits on old tree, Sidon, Lebanon.

ute wasps. Inside the flask-shaped syconium are the unisexual flowers, stripped of all color and display. Some of the pistillate (female) flowers have long styles; others have short styles. The commensal relationship between insects and flowers is essential to the existence of both organisms. Today, however, many varieties of figs (both the common fig and the sycomore fig) are parthenocarpic: they can produce fruits without the benefit of insects.

An intriguing reference is made to the sycomore fig and its culture by the prophet Amos: " 'I am not a prophet,' Amos replied to [King] Amaziah, 'nor do I belong to a prophetic brotherhood. I am merely a herdsman and dresser of sycomore-figs' " (Amos 7:14, NJB). Specifically what is the role of a dresser of sycomore figs, like Amos? With a sharp knife he would gash the developing fruits about four days before harvest. The cut releases ethylene gas and stimulates fruit production without fertilization. Such gashes are present on sycomore figs retrieved from Egyptian tombs of the eleventh century BC (Galil 1968). Zaleman (1980) gives linguistic support to "gasher" rather than gatherer or dresser of the developing fruit.

Gashing was a way to ripen fruit without the involvement of insects, bypassing one of the most elegant plant-insect relationships. The wasp that fertilizes the sycomore fig, *Ceratosolen arabicus*, is dependent on the sycomore fig. Likewise, the sycomore fig, unless it is parthenocarpic, will not produce fruit without the wasp. The deceivingly drab syconium is actually a chamber for many activities, including wasp mating, gas exchange, wasp egg hatching, and fruit development—all with elegant timing beginning with a female wasp entering the syconium. When she enters, covered with pollen from visiting previous flowers, she pushes aside the scales that occlude the ostiole, the small opening at the top of the syconium. Once inside, she lays eggs only in the short-styled flowers, allowing the long-styled flowers to produce seed because they are not damaged.

As the syconium develops, the carbon dioxide level increases in the closed chamber. The first wasps to hatch are male, which tolerate the higher carbon dioxide level. They drill through the wall of the ovaries to mate with the female wasps, which have developed from the eggs laid in the flowers, and then proceed to make a hole in the syconium wall. With the ingress of air through the opening to the outside, the carbon dioxide level inside the syconium falls. This stimulates the gravid females to break out of the flowers and allows them to fly to another syconium, where the drama is repeated. The altruistic male wasps simply die within the syconium or fall to the ground.

The sycomore is native to East Africa but was brought to the Nile Valley (Galil 1977), where it was used for boats, sculpture, and coffins (Meiggs 1982), as well as for food. Then the tree was probably introduced to the Middle East thousands of years ago.

Sycomore was widely planted in Israel in Bible times: "And the king made silver to be in Jerusalem as stones, and cedars made he to be as the sycamore trees that are in the vale, for abundance" (I Kings 10:27, KJV; II Chronicles 1:15, 9:27). King David had a royal grove of the trees: "Baal-Hanan the Gederite was in charge of the olive and sycamore-fig trees in the western foothills" (I Chronicles 27:28, NIV). Today, few large trees remain. Most have been cut to make coffins, since the sycomore fig is one of the few trees in the region to obtain sufficient girth for this use. For this reason, sycomore wood was also valuable for ship timbers, sculpture, and sarcophagi (Meiggs 1982).

The best-known sycomore in the Bible is the one mentioned in Luke 19, climbed by the unpopular tax gatherer, Zacchaeus. There are numerous large sycomore trees in present-day Jericho, but the tree singled out for display to tourists as Zacchaeus's tree is about 2000 years too young, and it is not *Ficus sycomorus*.

Because sycomore is one of the largest trees in the region, it is a symbol of something established and difficult to move: "He [Jesus] replied, 'If you have faith as small as a mustard seed, you can say to this mulberry [*sukaminos*] tree, "Be uprooted and planted in the sea," and it will obey you'" (Luke 17:6, NLT). This verse is best understood by knowing that the "mulberry," or more accurately "sycamine" (KJV) or "sycamore" (MSG), can be a large tree. This fits the imagery of the mountain—a large object for faith to overcome.

The fruits of *Ficus sycomorus* are no longer important commercially, although I have eaten sycomore figs sold in the market in Gaza, and the fruits are collected by local residents in Sidon, Lebanon. The taste is pleasant and sweet. They are considerably smaller than the common fig, but were once widely eaten.

Tamarisk

J UST ABOUT THE ONLY TREES THAT inhabit the shores of the Dead Sea and other hypersaline regions in the Middle East are species of tamarisk. Like some other desert shrubs and trees, tamarisks have incredibly long taproots, capable of extending meters into the desert soil to obtain water.

Tamarix is common in the Arabian Peninsula and throughout the Middle East. The leaves are tiny, scale-like, and crowded. On the leaves there are glands that actively secrete salt from the soil. During the day,

Tamarisk leaves secrete salt, near the Dead Sea.

the plants secrete salt, and at night the salt absorbs water, which evaporates in the morning sun, cooling anyone sleeping under it. For this reason, tamarisks are sought-after shade trees in the desert.

Flowers are small and often pink, their large masses forming attractive sprays. The ripe capsules release seeds with long hairs that aid in distribution. Two species are frequent in the Middle East: *Tamarix aphylla* and *T. nilotica*. The number of species and species delineation are unclear.

The wood of tamarisk is hard and durable. Trunks of tamarisk were used in the fortifications of Masada (Liphschitz et al. 1981), no doubt

A large tamarisk shrub in a wadi near Wadi Mujib, Jordan. Like the tamarisk, the date palm (in the distance) can also survive in areas with high salt concentration.

Tamarisk trees on the shore of the Dead Sea near Ein Gedi, Israel.

because this tree is one of the few woody plants of any size in the Dead Sea region.

The Hebrew word for tamarisk is *eshel*, cognate with *athl* in the Quran, where the habitat of tamarisk is clearly indicated. A verse records the judgment of a city by the destruction of a dam, which leads to desertification, and in place of gardens come thornbush and tamarisks: "There was a sign for the people of Saba in their habitations: Two gardens, on the right and left. (And they were told) 'Eat of what your Lord has given you and be thankful. Fair is your land, and forgiving your Lord.' But they turned away. So we let loose on them the inundation of (the dyke of) Al-'rim, replacing their gardens with two other gardens which bore only bitter gourd, and tamarisks and a few spare lote trees" (Sura 34:15–16, Ali).

Two woody plants are mentioned in Genesis 21. The first is the shrub under which Hagar placed Ishmael (Genesis 21:15). The second is the tamarisk planted by Abraham: "Then Abraham planted a tamarisk [Hebrew *eshel*] tree at Beersheba, and there he worshipped the LORD, the Eternal God" (Genesis 21:33–34, NLT). The shrub could also easily be a tamarisk, since it is one of the most common shrubs and trees in the vicinity of Beersheba. In addition, it is rhizomatous and rapidly spreading, one reason tamarisk species have become such pests in other parts of the world.

Why did Abraham plant a tamarisk? Trees were often used as memorials for great men. It is therefore appropriate that Abraham should honor God by planting the tamarisk. It would be a permanent memorial of the covenant between the two.

Saul held court under a tamarisk in Gibeah: "Now Saul heard that David and his men had been discovered. And Saul, spear in hand, was seated under the tamarisk [*eshel*] tree on the hill at Gibeah, with all his officials standing around him" (I Samuel 22:6, NIV). This dark green tree would be evident from the hilltop and could probably be seen for miles, providing a sort of "address" for visitors. This tamarisk was likely a planted tree, since Gibeah is in the Mountains of Judea (now a suburb of Jerusalem), where tamarisks are not native. In I Samuel 31:13, Saul is buried under a tamarisk tree, while in I Chronicles 10:12 (JND), the reference is to a pistacia, or terebinth, tree. This apparent discrepancy can be explained by the fact that the word for tamarisk can also be translated as "grove," or perhaps the verse simply means "a large tree."

Tamarisk could be visiting an area near you. Several species have been introduced in arid and semiarid regions and are becoming aggressive because of their fecundity and ability to grow in waste areas.

Tares

The tares, in this case *Lolium temulentum*, are the narrower grains. The wheat, the wider grains, is a variety of durum and is larger than grains of emmer wheat, which was the most widely cultivated wheat in ancient times.

"SEPARATING WHEAT FROM TARES" is a common expression based on one of the better-known parables of Jesus. But what is this plant, *zizanion* in Greek, mentioned only in Matthew 13? The Greek word has been variously translated as tares, darnel, and simply weeds.

While agricultural weeds are cited in several verses in the Old Testament (Job 31:40; Proverbs 24:31; Hosea 10:4), weeding of crops is not mentioned in the Bible and was apparently not practiced for grain crops in Egypt (Murray 2000). The weeds were simply allowed to mature with the crop, like the tares, and were harvested along with the crop and used as fodder or fuel.

The two most likely candidates for tares are common segetals (weeds associated with crops) in the Middle East. The first is *Cephalaria syriaca*, related to the attractive garden scabiosa, which are grown for their colorful flowers (actually aggregations of flowers) and decorative fruiting heads. *Cephalaria syriaca* is restricted in its range, while the other candidate, *Lolium temulentum*, is found throughout much of the world both as a weed and a pasture crop. No grasses are known to be toxic, so it may seem surprising that *L. temulentum* has frequently been implicated in cattle poisoning and, rarely, human poisoning (Hammouda et al. 1988) due to the presence of a toxic microorganism.

Cephalaria syriaca, Syrian scabiosa, in a wheat field in June, near Medaba, Jordan. The developing fruits are formed at the same height as the grain.

Lolium temulentum, darnel, in May, near Latakia, Syria. The tares are the green stems.

Cephalaria syriaca is an annual that reaches a height of 1.3 meters (4 feet) with a single stem that branches to produce numerous heads of flowers. The flowers are much less attractive than those of many members of the family and produce a small, hard seed (technically a fruit) with a very bitter taste. Despite the bitterness, the fruit is not toxic and has potential as a source of vegetable oil (Yazicioğlu et al. 1978). In the Middle East, this plant is found in the driest places where wheat is grown.

On the other hand, darnel, *Lolium temulentum*, is a grass, which like *Cephalaria syriaca* grows to the same height as a mature wheat plant and is often found growing in wheat fields. The grains are similar in size to those of wheat. It is a classic segetal plant.

The association of tares with wheat requires a closer look in the spot where the plant is mentioned: "The Kingdom of Heaven is like a farmer who planted good seed in his field. But that night as the workers slept, his enemy came and planted weeds among the wheat, then slipped away. When the crop began to grow and produce grain, the weeds also grew. The farmer's workers went to him and said, 'Sir, the field where you planted that good seed is full of weeds! Where did they come from?' 'An enemy has done this!' the farmer exclaimed. 'Should we pull out the weeds?' they asked. 'No,' he replied, 'you'll uproot the wheat if you do. Let both grow together until the harvest. Then I will tell the harvesters to sort out the weeds, tie them into bundles, and burn them, and to put the wheat in the barn'" (Matthew 13:24–30, NLT).

Unlike the other six parables in this chapter, the following required unpacking by the Teacher: "Then, leaving the crowds outside, Jesus went into the house. His disciples said, 'Please explain to us the story of the weeds in the field.' Jesus replied, 'The Son of Man is the farmer who plants the good seed. The field is the world, and the good seed represents the people of the Kingdom. The weeds are the people who belong to the evil one. The enemy who planted the weeds among the wheat is the devil. The harvest is the end of the world, and the harvesters are the angels. Just as the weeds are sorted out and burned in the fire, so it will be at the end of the world. The Son of Man will send his angels, and they will remove from his Kingdom everything that causes sin and all who do evil. And the angels will throw them into the fiery furnace, where there will be weeping and gnashing of teeth. Then the righteous will shine like the sun in their Father's Kingdom. Anyone with ears to hear should listen and understand!'" (Matthew 13:36–43, NLT).

If this parable is to be understood, we have to scrutinize the text. First, tares are associated with wheat, not with the other dominant ancient grain, barley. Contamination of the seed is implied. And it is obvious that the weed has a life cycle that is synchronous with the wheat. Put another way, tares are segetal plants in wheat fields. When the wheat nears maturity it is clearly evident that the weed and the wheat plants can be distinguished. How does this background help us determine which plant is *zizanion*? There is evidence from indigenous peoples.

Local Arab farmers in Jordan, Lebanon, and Syria refer to a weed that grows with wheat by the Arabic name *zawan*. This pejorative word describes an undesirable weed associated with wheat (Musselman 2001). The weed is enshrined in a proverb, "The *zawan* of your own field is better than the wheat of the crusaders," often applied to people seeking wives from more distant places rather than their own villages. Greppin (1995) also states that *zawan* refers to *Lolium temulentum* in Arabic.

In Jordan, *zawan* is clearly *Cephalaria syriaca*. Farmers state unequivocally that it occurs only in wheat, not in barley. However, farmers in higher rainfall areas of Lebanon and Syria use the term *zawan* for *Lolium temulentum*. And other plants are also considered candidates for tares (Musselman 2001).

Translating *zizanion* as "thistle," as in the MSG, seems to miss the teaching of the parable that the intruder resembles or imitates the crop, which is certainly not the case with thistles.

Terebinth

Dried fruits of
Pistacia atlantica.

IT IS UNCLEAR FROM THE SCRIPTURES precisely which tree is indicated by the Hebrew word *elah* or one of its derivatives. For example, the tree under which King Saul was buried (in I Samuel 31:13) is given as "the green tree" (NIV), "oak" (KJV and NASB), and "terebinth" (JND). In I Chronicles 14:14, the same tree is called "balsam" (NIV) and "mulberry" (KJV and JND). Balsam may be used as a name because of a resin extracted from the tree.

So what is terebinth or, more correctly, pistacia? Three species occur in the Middle East: the Atlantic pistacia, *Pistacia atlantica*; terebinth, *P. terebinthus*; and the Palestine pistacia, *P. palaestina* (also known as *P. terebinthus* var. *palaestina*). Atlantic pistacia is the largest of the three trees and therefore is assumed to be the one in the scriptures, although it is not possible to precisely name the species.

There are several well-defined forest types in the Middle East. Species of the genus *Pistacia* comprise an important group of trees in this guild of plants. A major Middle Eastern forest type is known as the oak-terebinth forest, because *Pistacia* species are such important components. Both *P. atlantica* and *P. palaestina* can be large trees with hard, durable wood valued for building and carpentry. Leaves are compound with an odd number of leaflets. These trees are unisexual, with small, inconspicuous flowers apparently wind pollinated. The small, hard fruits are sold as a condiment. Like all parts of the tree, the fruits con-

Degraded forest of *Pistacia khinjuk* in May, Jebel Abdel Aziz, northern Mesopotamia, Syria. This species of the genus grows in drier habitats than the other terebinths.

Craftsman with his spoons and pastry molds made from terebinth (white wood) and apricot (orange wood). Straight Street (Acts 9:11) in Damascus.

Pistacia atlantica in May, in the Hauran region of southeastern Syria. At one time, there were extensive forests of this species throughout much of the Middle East.

tain aromatic compounds. For this reason, they are sometimes placed under traditional flat bread during baking to provide a subtle flavor that reminds me of pine resin.

When undisturbed (a rare occurrence in the Middle East), the trees reach a very large size and can live up to 1000 years. In fact, the Atlantic pistacia is recorded as the largest tree in Israel in recent history (Danin 1979). Pistacia develops a deep and extensive root system and therefore remains green even in years of drought. It often sprouts from the stump after cutting, as noted in this Bible verse: "And suppose one-tenth of them are left in it, that will be stripped again, like the terebinth, like the oak, cut back to the stock; their stock is a holy seed" (Isaiah 6:13, NJB).

Additional references to large trees, possibly pistacia trees, include: "And they gave to Jacob all the strange gods that were in their hand, and the rings that were in their ears, and Jacob hid them under the terebinth that [is] by Shechem" (Genesis 35:4, JND); "The Angel of Yahweh came and sat under the terebinth at Ophrah which belonged to Joash of Abiezer" (Judges 6:11, NJB); "All the valiant men arose, and took up the body of Saul and the bodies of his sons, and brought them to Jabesh, and buried their bones under the terebinth of Jabesh, and fasted seven days" (I Chronicles 10:12, NJB; but see I Samuel 31:13); and, "He has cut down cedars, has selected an oak and a terebinth which he has grown for himself among the trees in the forest and has planted a pine tree which the rain has nourished" (Isaiah 44:14, NJB). Because of their large size and great age, pistacia trees were well-known landmarks and were used as memorials for the dead, a practice still followed in some Arab villages. But the pistacia trees also became the object of idolatry: "They offer sacrifice on the mountaintops, they burn incense on the hills, under oak and poplar and terebinth, for pleasant is their shade" (Hosea 4:13, NJB). Did Jacob bury the idols under the "oak" of Shechem because the tree was an object of veneration?

Again in the holy books great trees are often associated with great men. Gideon was by a large tree when he was called by God (Judges

6:11). David faced Goliath in the Valley of the Pistacias (I Samuel 17:2) (*elah* in Hebrew). Absalom, great in his own eyes, was trapped in a large pistacia: "And Absalom found himself in the presence of David's servants. And Absalom was riding upon a mule, and the mule went under the thick boughs of the great terebinth, and his head caught in the terebinth, and he was taken up between the Heaven and the earth; and the mule that was under him went away" (II Samuel 18:9, JND). A review of these verses in diverse translations reveals the various ways this tree is treated. Ultimately, it is not possible to discern whether oak or terebinth is indicated.

The small, hard fruits of *Pistacia palaestina* are sold in Arab markets as a condiment and are sometimes a component of *za'atar*, a spicy mix put on bread.

Insect galls formed on the trees have been harvested for tannin for tanning animal hides and sometimes for medicinal use (Flamini et al. 2004).

An especially interesting feature of the genus *Pistacia* is the presence of oils and a fragrant resin with a smell resembling that of turpentine. (The source of our English word "turpentine" is derived from the word for terebinth.) Today, turpentine is derived from pine trees, but in ancient times terebinth was the source of a compound used in a similar manner. The famed balm of Gilead is likely the resin of this tree. I like the suggestion of Whiston (n.d.) that "balm of Gilead" would be better named "turpentine of Gilead."

Because of the powerful, attractive imagery of the reference in Jeremiah, the term "balm of Gilead" has entered English in a variety of ways. One of the most interesting to me is in the naming of plants. A widespread species of poplar is *Populus balsamifera*, which grows in the northern United States, Canada, and Alaska. The tree has resinous, sticky buds that have a strong, fragrant odor, and on a hot, summer day the odor fills the air. At one time, the dried buds were marketed as "balm of Gilead" and sold to make a decoction as a remedy for various maladies.

As recorded by Moldenke and Moldenke (1952), the most probable source for the true, biblical, balm of Gilead is *Pistacia lentiscus*. The first mention of this balm is associated with the story of Joseph. Rather than kill Joseph, his brothers sold him to "a caravan of Ishmaelites coming from Gilead. Their camels were loaded with spices, balm [Hebrew *tsory*] and myrrh, and they were on their way to take them down to Egypt" (Genesis 37:25). "Is their no balm [*tsory*] in Gilead?" asks the weeping prophet in Jeremiah 8:22. The same word, *tsory*, is used later in Jeremiah: "Go up to Gilead and fetch balm, virgin daughter of Egypt!" (Jeremiah 46:11a, NJB); and, "Babylon has suddenly fallen, is broken: wail for her! Fetch balm for her wounds, perhaps she can be cured!" (Jeremiah 51:8, NJB). And in Ezekiel: "Judah and Israel traded with you; they exchanged wheat from Minnith and confections, honey, oil and balm for your wares" (Ezekiel 27:17, NIV). In all these verses, the resin of a *Pistacia* species fits well, as does its destination, Egypt.

This resin is now known to be one of the materials used in preparation of mummies in ancient Egypt (Columbini et al. 2000, Buckley and Evershed 2001). The antibacterial activity of *Pistacia lentiscus* var. *chio* has recently been studied, indicating why it might have value in mummification, though the species of *Pistacia* for mummification is not certain (Serpico 2000). Resin from *P. lentiscus* from the Greek island of Chio, an ancient and well-documented source, is known as mastic (Langenheim 2003). Since *Pistacia* trees are not native to Egypt, resin was imported from Gilead and contiguous regions.

The appeal of balm of Gilead is well expressed in the old spiritual: "There is a balm in Gilead / to make the wounded whole. / There is a balm in Gilead / to heal the sin sick soul."

Thistle

Thistle, *Echinops* species, in July, near Wadi Mousa, southern Jordan.

I N MUCH OF THE MIDDLE EAST, thistle is the most conspicuous vegetation along roads and in fields. At the edge of barley and wheat fields, a painful border of thistles guards the harvest. Roadsides are often thickets of thistles. In fact, thistles and other armed plants are so common in this part of the world that if you sent a first-time visitor on a hike through fields, she or he would quickly get the point.

No wonder these succulent and often delicious plants need protection. The entire countryside, including urban areas, is grazed by goats and sheep. If a plant is not toxic or armed, it ends up as a meal!

The Old Testament (Hebrew) word for thistle, *chowach*, is cognate with the modern Arabic *shawk*, thorn. The word is sometimes translated as thorn or thistle, as in the first reference to armed plants in the Bible: "Cursed is the ground for thy sake; in sorrow shalt thou eat of it all the days of thy life; thorns also and thistles shall it bring forth to thee; and thou shalt eat the herb of the field" (Genesis 3:17–18, KJV). The word translated "thorn" is *qots*. Thus, the two words *chowach* and *qots* (as well as several others) can be translated as thistle or thorn.

The Genesis account is a helpful commentary on the ecology of thistles. The plant is usually associated with disturbed areas like fields and roadsides. Scripture provides several examples: "I went past the field of the sluggard, past the vineyard of the man who lacks judgment;

Onopordum species in barley field in May near ruins of ancient Aroer (Joshua 12:2).

Onopordum species flowering head in May, near Deir Attaya, Syria. Despite fierce armament, insects often cause extensive damage to species of this genus of thistles.

thorns had come up everywhere, the ground was covered with weeds, and the stone wall was in ruins" (Proverbs 24:30–31, NIV). The "thorns" are probably thistles, since a woody plant would not grow as fast as an annual plant. Thistles are annual, armed plants.

In one of the best-known thistles, the garden artichoke, the leaf-like structures that surround the flower head are tipped with a sharp point. When eating the artichoke, we remove the outer "leaves" until we get to the center of the immature flower head, the heart of the artichoke. If allowed to flower, the artichoke would be a large, beautiful flower. Wild relatives of the cultivated artichoke are common in the Middle East and often have horrific prickles on the flower head 3 centimeters (about 1 inch) long. These prickles discouraged me from testing the culinary value of the plant. When young, the flower heads of a wild relative of artichoke resemble an old-fashioned shaving brush, giving it one of its common names in Arabic, "the donkey's shaving brush," because of its brush-like flower heads and impressive armor.

Thistles are nonwoody plants that are outfitted with prickles, one of the three different kinds of plant armor recognized by botanists. Thorns are modified branches. Spines are modified leaves. Both are most common on trees and shrubs or perennial plants. Prickles are sharp projections that may arise from any plant surface—like those of the artichoke and "donkey's shaving brush." Prickles are formed on the leaves, stems, and even the flower heads while the plants are young and most susceptible to grazing.

Most thistles belong to the sunflower family. Individual flowers of the sunflower family are very small, seldom more than a few millimeters (⅛ inch) wide. But hundreds can be produced in a solitary flowering head. Each flower produces a single-seeded fruit, commonly referred to as a seed. Fruits may have specialized adaptations for airborne dispersal. Long, soft hairs ("down") on the fruits allow them to be lifted by the dry winds of summer and widely scattered. I am always intrigued at the incongruity of soft thistle down caught in the sharp prickles of the plant. The seeds can remain dormant in the soil, and when the area is plowed or disturbed, the seeds are exposed to light and water and germinate.

Several thistles are edible. In fact, some wild relatives of lettuce (species in the genus *Lactuca*), common in the Middle East, are armed. Another is safflower (*Carthamus tinctorius*), known in Arabic as *zafran* because the flowers are collected, dried, and used to color rice—like true saffron.

In addition to the plants I have mentioned, there are many other genera of thistles, including representatives of the genera *Onopordum*, *Echinops*, *Silybum*, and *Atractylis*. Thistles are abundant and diverse in western Asia. Some *Echinops* species have been marketed for their horticultural value. *Silybum marianum* is perhaps the most widespread and abundant thistle at the margin of roads and agricultural fields. Thistle's frequency is enhanced by grazing animals, which, avoiding the thistles' armor, favor other plants, allowing thistles to get the upper hand. Few groups of plants would make a more lasting impression on a visitor than these.

Echinops flowers in July, near Ajlon, Jordan.

Thornbush

Spines of thornbush.

"THOSE ON THE RIGHT HAND—happy shall be those on the right hand! They shall recline on couches raised on high in the shade of thornless sidres and clusters of talh; amidst gushing waters and abundant fruits, unforbidden, never-ending" (Sura 56:27–33, Dawood; Ali translates *sidr* as *lote*). The identity of "thornless sidres" remains controversial. Farooqi (2003), for example, claims that this is cedar of Lebanon, based on the availability of suitable habitat for cedar in Yemen. This assertion is figurative because Yemen is outside the known range of cedar of Lebanon and also because the cedar is unarmed, in contrast to thornbush in nature (not in Paradise), which is armed. The best match is *Ziziphus spina-christi*, or a related species. *Sidr* is the name used for species of *Ziziphus* in Saudi Arabia (Chaudhary 2001). It is sometimes called *lote* in quranic literature.

Thornbush is also mentioned in the Bible, and, again, its true identity is debatable. In the first botanical discourse in the Bible, by Jotham on Mount Gerazim (modern-day Nablus), five trees are mentioned: cedar of Lebanon, olive, fig, grape, and thornbush (sometimes translated as bramble): "One day the trees went out to anoint a king for themselves. They said to the olive tree, 'Be our king.' But the olive tree answered, 'Should I give up my oil, by which both gods and men are honored, to hold sway over the trees?' Next, the trees said to the fig tree, 'Come and be our king.' But the fig tree replied, 'Should I give

This thornbush tree is an exceptionally large specimen, in May, in the vicinity of Sair, near Hebron. The size is evident by the man at the left.

Thornbush has specialized stipules (leaf bases) that are spines. In November, Tigray State, Ethiopia.

Thornbush fruits are collected and eaten fresh or dried. The flavor is sweet but insipid.

up my fruit, so good and sweet, to hold sway over the trees?' Then the trees said to the vine, 'Come and be our king.' But the vine answered, 'Should I give up my wine, which cheers both gods and men, to hold sway over the trees?' Finally all the trees said to the thornbush, 'Come and be our king.' The thornbush said to the trees, 'If you really want to anoint me king over you, come and take refuge in my shade; but if not, then let fire come out of the thornbush and consume the cedars of Lebanon!'" (Judges 9:8–15, NIV).

The most likely plant for thornbush, *Ziziphus spina-christi*, is a common component of the steppe vegetation in that region, where olives, figs, and grapes are also grown. Thus, it comports well with both the ecology of the region and the literary image of a valueless tree.

Sidr (or *lote*) is a straggly shrub or small tree that thrives in areas of low rainfall. The plants are viciously armed with specialized stipules (modified leaf bases) in a curious way: at each leaf base one of the spines is straight, the other is curved. Often the only tree in the semi-desert, *lote* is sought out for its shade. This image is the one in Paradise quoted here, with the tree blessed by being thornless. In one of the Hadiths (sayings of the Prophet Mohammad), a decoction of *sidr* leaves is used to wash a corpse before burial, a custom still followed by Muslims in some areas of the Middle East.

Flowers are small, yellowish green, and can appear any time of year. The fruits are about the size of a small olive and are edible. In fact, some species of the genus, notably *Ziziphus lotus*, are grown for their fruit; the fruit of *Z. lotus* is known in English as jujube. While it is considered a delicacy in the Middle East, I find the taste reminiscent of a mealy apple.

Thornbush is a common, well-known component of the flora of western Asia. Because of its edible fruits, it would be readily identified in scriptures.

Thyine

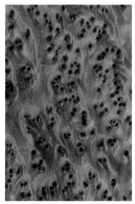

Polished piece of wood of thyine, *Tetraclinis articulata*, from the underground portion of the tree.

THE BIBLE PROVIDES INSIGHT INTO which objects were highly valued in those epochs. Most are well known— gold, silver, various gemstones. Among the least known today is thyine, *Tetraclinis articulata*, a plant found in only one verse: "She [Babylon] bought great quantities of gold, silver, jewels, and pearls; fine linen, purple, silk, and scarlet cloth; things made of fragrant thyine wood, ivory goods, and objects made of expensive wood; and bronze, iron, and marble" (Revelation 18:11–12, NLT).

These luxury goods, including thyine wood, were traded in Babylon, a city symbolic of materialism and hedonism. "Thyine" is the transliteration of the Greek *thuinos* and therefore the translation preferred over "citron wood" (NIV, NKJV), "perfumed wood" (NLT), or "scented wood" (RSV).

While currently unfamiliar, thyine wood was well known in the ancient Mediterranean world. It is one of the most beautiful woods in the world. People living in New Testament times would recognize thyine as a wood used to make furniture for the rich and powerful, consonant with its inclusion in a list of luxury items. As Pliny put it so clearly: "Few things that supply the apparatus of a more luxurious life rank with this tree" (Rackham 2000). Pliny probably had *Tetraclinus articulata* in mind when he wrote that the outstanding feature of the wood, derived as he rightly notes from the underground portion of the tree, had "wavy marks forming a vein or else little spirals"; and,

Thyine tree in October, in
a preserve near Tamara,
Morocco. The persistent
low branches suggest that
this tree is part of a fire-
maintained plant community.

Worker ready to cut thyine
trunk, in Essaouira, Morocco,
which is the center of
the artisan industry for
working this wood.

"Some have wavy crinkled markings, which are more esteemed if they resemble the eyes in a peacock's tail" (Rackham 2000, Kaiser 1997). In Homer's *Odyssey*, the alluring Calypso burns thyine in her fireplace, which is referred to by Pliny in his review of the tree's history. As they are today, beautiful tables were inlaid with thyine; Pliny recorded one that was sold at the price of a large estate.

The thyine tree is a small gymnosperm native to North Africa. Theophrastus noted it growing in the district of Cyrene, modern-day Libya, where it was extirpated by overharvesting and urban sprawl (Hughes 1983). Today, the largest stands of *T. articulata* are found in the Atlas Mountains of Morocco, with outlier populations in Algeria, Spain, and a small stand in Malta (Buhagiar et al. 2000). About 10 percent of present forest cover in Morocco is thyine, known in Moroccan Arabic as *araar*; most of this forest is on government land. The center of the *araar* industry is the city of Essaouira on the Atlantic Ocean, with the largest extant trees being in the vicinity of Agadir in southern Morocco.

Two types of wood are extracted from the tree. The choice wood is from the underground portion, where numerous buds create a bird's-eye pattern. The aerial portion of the tree provides timber that is easy to work, strong, but unremarkable in color.

The tree can reach a height of 10 meters (30 feet), with a crown typical of many gymnosperms—conical when mature. Pollen cones and seed cones are produced on the same tree. An unusual feature of thyine culture is coppicing: the stems are cut and the trees resprout from the root.

Resin, known as *sandarac*, is extracted from the tree (Langenheim 2003). The resin is implied in the translation of thyine as "fragrant wood" in some Bible versions. Stems are incised, allowing the resin to exude and harden; it is then collected. This practice of cutting the trees to extract *sandarac* was outlawed in Morocco more than 50 years ago. *Sandarac* was used in preparing mummies (Colombini et al. 2000) and was widely traded in ancient times.

Tumbleweed

TUMBLEWEED OR *GUNDELIA TOUR-nefortii* is a common plant in the steppe regions of Bible lands. It is mentioned in the Bible: "Make them like tumbleweed [Hebrew *galgal*], O my God, like chaff before the wind" (Psalm 83:13, NIV). Some scholars think that the tumbleweed in this verse is *akoub*, an Arabic name designating a heavily armed plant, a true thistle.

Closeup of tumbleweed with flowers, near Makawir, Jordan, the site of King Herod's palace.

The scriptures refer to the tumbling nature of the plant, which is similar in behavior to the famous tumbleweeds of the American Great Plains (*Salsola kali* and other species), which, when mature, break from their roots and dry, then roll along the landscape carried by the wind.

In the Middle East, in March, *akoub* plants are cut at the base and the prickles removed. The disarmed plants are relished as a delicacy that is cooked with meat or sauteed with oil and onions. After purchasing some *akoub*, tediously I removed the young but strong prickles with scissors. Then, I cooked it with a little olive oil. The flavor resembled mild broccoli. Like many wild foods, the appeal is in its wild origin and lore more than in its flavor. Harvesting has become so widespread that measures are being taken to protect the plant in Israel (Kaplan et al. 1995). After my experience preparing the delicacy with resultant bloody hands from the vicious spines and only a few strands to eat, I pose no threat to existing populations of *akoub*.

I purchased this box of
akoub from a young Bedouin
boy selling it along the
road near Jerash, Jordan.

By mid May, the *akoub* stem has separated from the root, allowing the entire plant to tumble, carried by the wind. Near Makawir, the location of Herod's palace east of the Jordan River and the likely site of the decapitation of John the Baptist, I found abundant *akoub*. As the thistle tumbles over the open ground, the fruits fall out. *Akoub*'s dispersal takes place about the same time as wheat harvest, "driven before the wind like chaff on the hills, like tumbleweed before a gale" (Isaiah 17:13, NIV).

Tumbleweed may not be the most desirable way to translate this plant because it is then likened to the well-known tumbleweeds of America's Great Plains. While ambulatory like its prairie counterpart, *akoub* has a different mechanism of separating from its base, and belongs to an unrelated family.

Walnut

The fruit, or "nut," of English or Persian walnut.

THE FRUIT OF THE ENGLISH WALNUT (*Juglans regia*) is more popular than that of the black walnut (*Juglans nigra*) because it is much easier to crack. And like the wood of black walnut, English walnut wood is highly valued: it is one of the woods used in producing the beautiful damascene furniture in which mother-of-pearl is inlaid into the walnut. But the walnut referenced only once in the Bible is likely mentioned because of its fertility symbolism.

Bible scholars generally agree that the nut trees mentioned in Song of Songs 6:11 are the trees known as English walnut, or more precisely as Persian walnut (also *Juglans regia*), which are cultivated in many parts of the world. The center of origin of this species is not known, but it is widely grown in the Middle East, where the seeds of the fruits, the "nuts," are frequent ingredients in pastries and candies. A unique delicacy in Syria is candied green walnut: in this sweet, the entire fruit is eaten, including the part that will become bony.

The walnut can grow to be a large, graceful tree. The dark green leaves and strong, thick trunk would tower over vines and shrubby pomegranates in the Middle East landscape. In ancient times, the walnut was a symbol of fertility. This image is consonant with the sensuous garden in Song of Songs: "My beloved has gone down to his garden, to the beds of balsam, to pasture his flock in the gardens and gather lilies" (Song of Songs 6:2, NASB), alluding to a garden of spices and lilies; and, "I went down to the orchard of nut trees to see the blossoms of the valley, to see whether the vine had budded or the pomegranates had bloomed" (Song of Songs 6:11, NASB), referring to a garden of nuts located in the valley and associated with grapes and pomegranates. Scripture speaks much of the grape (more than any other plant) and often of the pomegranate, but what does this mention of the walnut tell us? In line with the imagery of a sensuous garden, the walnut is appropriately positioned.

These developing walnuts are growing in a commercial walnut grove near Chico, California.

Watermelon

Watermelon is native to arid regions.

WATERMELON IS NOT A FOOD WE would readily associate with the desert. Yet watermelon, *Citrullus lanatus*, is native to sub-Saharan Africa, and the Children of Israel learned to love it. In fact, after leaving, in a fit of forgetfulness, they appeared ready to return even to bondage in order to have delicacies of Egypt, including melons: "We remember the fish which we used to eat free in Egypt, the cucumbers and the melons and the leeks and the onions and the garlic" (Numbers 11:5, NASB). Watermelon is actually one of two melons they missed;, the other resembled a cucumber.

At the border of the Sahara Desert, we can still find wild watermelons, though they bear little resemblance to the behemoths now sold in markets. These African melons are ball shaped, with a diameter of about 15 centimeters (6 inches). They have a smooth, thick rind, relatively little flesh, and numerous seeds. Because of the thickness of the rind, the melon keeps fresh for a long time. Seeds are edible; the roasted seeds are a common snack in Sudan, Egypt, and other countries. Watermelon is an annual vine with yellow flowers that trails along the ground. The edible part is the placenta of the fruit.

Murray (2000) cites workers who suggest that the remains identified as watermelon in Egyptian archaeology are actually the related *Citrullus colycinthis*. This idea seems unlikely because the colycinth tastes extremely bitter and may be toxic; its presence in tombs could have been for a medical use.

Watermelons in a market near Nahr el Kalb, Lebanon. Courtesy Houssam Shaiban.

Although native to sub-Saharan Africa, watermelon is among the most common summer fruits in the United States. This flowering vine with developing fruit is at the National Arboretum, Washington, DC.

Wheat

Emmer wheat in trial plots at the International Center for Agricultural Research in the Dry Areas near Aleppo, Syria.

H
UMAN CIVILIZATION RELIES ON only a few plants for existence, most notably on grains. Of these, rice is the most important, followed by wheat. People in western Asia depend on wheat for a variety of products, especially bread. Wheat played a critical role in the agrarian societies of the ancient Middle East. The Quran does not delineate which species are included in the term "grain." In the three references to grain, they are portrayed as a provision from God: "Let the once-dead earth be a sign for them. We gave it life, and from it produced grain for their sustenance" (Sura 36:33, Dawood). The Bible, on the other hand, distinguishes between wheat and barley.

Wheat, *khittaw* in Hebrew, is the most important of the "six species of the land": "It is a land of wheat and barley; of grapevines, fig trees, and pomegranates; of olive oil and honey" (Deuteronomy 8:8, NLT). Wheat is the most important plant because it provides the greatest amount of nutrition of the crops.

The Greek for "wheat" is *sitos*. The daily manifestation of this divine provision was bread, the best-known product of wheat, often synonymous with "food." As if to emphasize this point, Jesus said, "I am the bread of life," in His famous discourse in John 6:35. Bread in Bible days was very different from modern bread. In addition, grain, beer, straw, roasted green wheat, and chaff are also produced from the wheat plant and were widely used in Bible times.

Agricultural worker
examining durum wheat
in May, near Tubas,
Palestinian Territories.

Flour was an essential element in many of the Levitical offerings. Straw was used for fodder, bedding of animals, basketry, roofing thatch, and to make bricks. Chaff, the remains after threshing and winnowing grain, is often used in the scriptures as the symbol of utter worthlessness. These uses of wheat are often overlooked by modern-day Bible readers.

Understanding the significance of the many uses of wheat requires some background on the plant—its culture and its evolution. Why is this apparently simple plant the basis of human subsistence in so many parts of the world? What are the major groups of wheat? What wheats were used in the ancient Middle East?

Wheat—like barley, rye, maize (corn), rice, and oats—is a cereal. Cereals are all annual grasses, members of one of the largest families of flowering plants, the Poaceae (also known as the Graminae). Through millennia, wild cereal plants were modified by artificial selection for cultivation: farmers would save the seed of plants with desirable qualities. One such quality is tillering, the ability to produce additional stems from the base of the plant. Anyone who has sown sweet corn in a home garden has seen tillering: put three seeds (kernels) of corn in the ground and four or five stems emerge. These extra stems, each of which can produce ears (or heads), are "tillers." More stems and more heads result in more grain per plant.

At first appearance, the fruiting head of wheat looks bewildering in complexity, with lots of small, carefully engineered parts. But the basic plan is simple. Each flower (floret) is surrounded by small, modified leaves (bracts). Inconspicuous and tiny, the flower has all necessary reproductive equipment. Flowers, in turn, are grouped into spikelets. Every spikelet is also surrounded by protective bracts, called glumes. Collectively, these diverse bracts form the chaff, which must be separated from the grain.

The head of the grain, then, is an aggregation of florets arranged in spikelets. Wheat, like all cereals, produces a specialized fruit, the grain, in which the coat of the fruit and the coat of the seed are fused. This feature gives extra protection to the seed and allows storage through dry or cold seasons, facilitating sedentary (settled) agriculture. Each grain consists of a minute embryo (the germ), a large amount of starch (the endosperm), and the fruit coat (bran). In modern white bread flour, the germ and bran have been removed; it is considerably less nutritious than whole-grain flour.

When mature, the wheat is cut (harvested), and then it is threshed (beaten or pounded to remove the grain). The condition of the bracts after threshing defines two major groups of wheats—the hulled wheats and the free-threshing wheats. Virtually all wheat grown in western Asia in ancient times was hulled wheat.

In hulled wheat, the glumes separate from the heads at threshing but remain attached to the grain. The product of threshing, then, is the grain with the attached glumes. With glumes in place, the wheat cannot be prepared for eating, so the grain must be further processed to release it from the glumes. Free-threshing wheats, on the other hand, have grains that readily separate from the glumes; the glumes stay with the head. So threshing of free-threshing wheat produces grain ready for milling. Most modern wheats are free threshing. Hulled wheats are not grown on a large commercial scale, today. Modern bread wheat and its processing are much different from the hulled wheats and their processing in Bible days.

"Shattering" is a feature of wild wheats: the grains fall from the plant as they ripen. The term refers to the shattering of the head when the wheat stem is cut at harvest and the grains fall and are lost. Shattering wheats are therefore of little agricultural value. The wheat produced in ancient times in the Middle East was hulled, free-threshing wheat. The product of harvesting was grain that separated freely from the plant but was still enclosed by glumes (or hulled).

Wheat originated in the northern reaches of Bible lands, the Fertile Crescent. Therein lies a mystery. During the first half of the twentieth century, scientists from several countries tracked the relatives of native wheats in the Fertile Crescent and surrounding areas, from the Caucasus Mountains to Mount Hermon. Like fingerprints, the chromosomes were used for identification of the various characters.

Through extensive searching in the field and by thorough laboratory studies, the genetic lineage of wheat—from modern bread wheat to the original wild relatives—was worked out. In recent years, this lineage has been documented and reconfirmed with powerful molecular techniques. Thus, the four ancestors of modern wheats have been identified: einkorn, emmer wheat, durum wheat, and bread wheat.

Wild einkorn (*Triticum monococcum*) is still common in the Fertile Crescent; it is a shattering grain, so it was of little value in cultivation in Bible days and probably was only harvested incidentally. Einkorn grains have been found at archaeological sites, apparently collected in the wild. From wild einkorn, prehistoric farmers selected for nonshattering plants and for wheats that produced grains maturing at the same time. The first wheat to be widely domesticated was emmer (*Triticum dicoccum*). Emmer is a hulled wheat. With continued domestication of emmer, durum wheat arose. Durum, *Triticum durum*, the modern source of semolina flour, is free threshing. Then, after hybridization between durum wheat and a wild grass, bread wheat appeared on the scene long before Christ. With a high gluten content, which traps carbon dioxide in bread dough and causes the dough to rise, bread wheat, *Triticum aestivum*, is the favored grain for making the light and fluffy loaves now favored in the West.

The selection and evolution of bread wheat, from einkorn through emmer and durum, is one of the best-documented examples of the evolution of any crop (Zohary and Hopf 2000). This study is an elegant model for studying other plants that have been cultivated since prehistoric times. What concerns us, however, are ancient wheats: which wheats were grown in Bible days?

The majority of wheat cultivated in Bible days was emmer, a type of hulled wheat. The presence of emmer wheat is implied from the biblical texts referring to threshing floors, threshing sledges, and mortars. Hulled emmer wheat required considerable work to extract the grain, which may be the reason why threshing sledges were widely used in Bible times, though wheat was threshed in other ways as well.

Although laborious to prepare, hulled wheats store well and are more resistant to insect damage than free-threshing wheats.

The use of a mortar and pestle to thresh hulled wheats is well known from a variety of archeobotanical studies. This specific use of the mortar and pestle was probably implied in this verse: "You cannot separate fools from their foolishness, even though you grind them like grain with mortar and pestle" (Proverbs 27:22, NLT). Some sort of mortar was also used by the Children of Israel in the wilderness, implying that mortars were essential household tools and that the wheat used in Egypt had to be pounded: "The manna looked like small coriander seeds, and it was pale yellow like gum resin. The people would go out and gather it from the ground. They made flour by grinding it with hand mills or pounding it in mortars" (Numbers 11:7–8, NLT).

After emmer wheat spikelets are pounded to remove the hulls, bread can be made from it, though it may not conform to our modern image of bread because its lower gluten content would make a flatter loaf. The gluten content of emmer is similar to that of barley, which also makes a flat loaf.

Very little of the wheat grown in Bible days was durum wheat. Why its cultivation was so limited is a mystery (Murray 2000a), since it is known from archaeological sites in Turkey from equivalent ages. Durum is also used to make bulghur, or *burghul*, cracked wheat widely used in Middle East cooking, as well as *frikeh*, roasted green wheat. Durum boiled in milk can be eaten as a kind of porridge. Bread can be made from it, although it does not contain as much gluten as bread wheat. It is the wheat of choice for making traditional Middle East flat bread. It also has the advantage of being free threshing and very productive. Having considered durum and emmer, we are left with the third kind of wheat in the Bible, spelt.

Spelt is a hulled bread wheat. The Hebrew word *kuccemeth* is translated as "spelt" in three places: "The flax and barley were destroyed, since the barley had headed and the flax was in bloom. The wheat and spelt, however, were not destroyed, because they ripen later" (Exodus 9:31–32, NIV); "When he has leveled the surface, does he not sow caraway and scatter cumin? Does he not plant wheat in its place, barley in its plot, and spelt in its field?" (Isaiah 28:25, NIV); and, "Take wheat and barley, beans and lentils, millet and spelt; put them in a storage jar and use them to make bread for yourself. You are to eat it during the 390 days you lie on your side" (Ezekiel 4:9a, NIV). *Kuccemeth* is rendered as "rie" in Exodus and Isaiah in the KJV and as "fitches" in Ezekiel; the NIV translates this word as "spelt."

The reference in Exodus 9:32, "The wheat and spelt, however, were not destroyed, because they ripen later," clearly distinguishes between the two crops damaged by the seventh plague, hail. But is the biblical spelt really true spelt, *Triticum spelta*? This seems unlikely because the wheat in the ancient Middle East was emmer and the distribution of spelt was limited; unlike most cultivated wheats, spelt may not have arisen in the Fertile Crescent. In fact, Murray (2000) states, "Contrary to popular belief, Egyptians did not grow spelt wheat." The Children of Israel had mortars in their households after leaving Egypt. This does not mean that the refugees took *kuccemeth* with them because the mortars would be needed for emmer. If there was no true spelt in ancient Egypt, what is *kuccemeth*? It is probably not einkorn, because this wheat matures later than emmer (Troccoli and Codianni 2005).

Kuccemeth is likely some race of wheat distinguished by color or another feature, distinctions commonly made by variation within crops by farmers and agriculturalists of all eras. We just do not know which variety it is. Mentioned very few times, it must be distinct from the widely planted emmer wheat. Also, in the Ezekiel account, *kuccemeth* is associated with food for the very poor. Does this make einkorn a candidate? Perhaps *kuccemeth* was free-threshing bread wheat or a specialized wheat that is no longer grown. What this apparent cereal is remains a mystery.

In the Bible lands of the Near East, cereals are sown in December and harvested after six or seven months. Wheat is grown in regions of high rainfall and fertile soil. Traditionally, farmers save wheat seeds from their harvest to sow the next crop. Jesus used allusions to sowing grain in His teaching, for example in prefiguring His resurrection: "Truly, truly, I say to you, unless a grain of wheat falls into the earth and dies, it remains by itself alone; but if it dies it bears much fruit" (John 12:24, NASB). A seed is planted. If it is not planted, it does not grow. If it does grow, it produces prodigiously. Was Jesus referring to tillering in this verse?

Depending on rainfall in the Middle East, barley would be harvested in mid May and wheat about one month later. The wheat harvest takes place long after the rains have ended, so that the sending of rain during the harvest was a manifest judgment from God: "Now therefore, stand and see this great thing which the Lord will do before your eyes: Is today not the wheat harvest? I will call to the Lord, and He will send thunder and rain, that you may perceive and see that your wickedness is great, which you have done in the sight of the Lord, in asking a king for yourselves" (I Samuel 12:16–17, NKJV). Rain at harvest time would cause the wheat plants to lodge (fall and mat together), making harvest difficult and decay of the crop likely.

Wheat is harvested in two ways. It can be cut, usually by a sickle or scythe, and then gathered in bundles. If fodder is scarce due to poor rainfall, the plant is pulled up to increase food for animals. Harvest is the cutting (or pulling) of the wheat, and threshing is the physical pounding or other mechanical abrasion of the heads to obtain the grain. Removing the glumes is the last stage of threshing with hulled wheats. Winnowing is the final cleaning of the grain. Harvesting yields sheaves, threshing yields grain, and winnowing yields chaff.

There were at least two methods of threshing grain with oxen in Bible days. The first, still widely practiced in Pakistan and Ethiopia, simply involves the oxen, usually yoked in a pair, trampling the grain on a threshing floor as referred to by the prophet Micah: "But they do not know the LORD's thoughts or understand his plan. These nations do not know that he is gathering them together to be beaten and trampled like sheaves of grain on a threshing floor" (Micah 4:12, NLT).

Harvesting wheat in June, near Medaba, Jordan. Workers are pulling the crop so that the entire plant can be used for fodder, a frequent practice in countries like Jordan that have a shortage of fodder. Sheaf of wheat in June, from field near Kerak, Jordan.

A second method involved a threshing sledge, or tribulum (Ataman 1999, Hillman 1981). The sledge was a platform of flat boards, sometimes with an upturned front end like a toboggan. Stones or metal spikes were affixed to the lower surface. The threshing sledge was drawn by an animal and weighted with stones (or children). As the sledge went over the wheat, the spikelets or grains would be abraded and removed from the stems. Often, the ox was tied to a stake or tree as it carried out its work, a familiar image to Bible audiences in both the Old and New Testaments: "You must not muzzle an ox to keep it from eating as it treads out the grain" (Deuteronomy 25:4, NLT); and in the New Testament, "Elders who do their work well should be respected and paid well, especially those who work hard at both preaching and teaching. For the scripture says, 'You must not muzzle an ox to keep it from eating as it treads out the grain'" (I Corinthians 9:9, NLT); and another reference, "Those who work deserve their pay!" (I Timothy 5:17–18, NLT).

Wheat was threshed on areas of flat rock where the grain could be spread out. Or flat areas were covered with clay to produce a smooth surface known as a threshing floor. Community gatherings were held at these places, perhaps because the relatively flat surface provided a sort of outdoor arena. Threshing removed the spikelets from the heads or, in the case of hulled wheats, may have removed the glumes as well. If the wheat was stored without dehulling, mortars and pestles could be used to prepare the grain. Today modern machines are used for threshing in the Middle East, but the grain is often piled at sites that long served as threshing floors for sledges. I have not seen a traditional threshing sledge used in the region for almost 20 years.

For winnowing, the farmer would throw the threshed grain into the air so the wind could carry away the chaff. A shallow basket or woven mat was used to hold and catch the grain. The final step was to lift the grain, often with a type of fork that allows the chaff to blow away: "His winnowing-fan is in his hand; he will clear his threshing-floor and gather his wheat into his barn; but the chaff he will burn in a fire that will never go out" (Matthew 3:12, NJB; Luke 3:17).

Threshing wheat. This sight would have been a familiar one in Bible times, especially since emmer wheat was grown. In this scene in October in Ethiopia, the oxen are muzzled.

CERTAINLY THE BEST-KNOWN biblical reference to wheat and wheat products regards bread, with almost 300 references. Considering the setting of the Quran, it is not surprising that wheat bread is not specifically mentioned. In the Bible, lack of bread resulted in hunger and famine, sometimes as a divine judgment. Food was bread.

In traditional western Asian cultures where bread is the staple food, it is treated with care. Stale bread is not thrown out; it is used in some way.

The Bible says little about the details of baking bread, such as the type of ovens that were used. Samuel (2000) provides helpful discussion on the baking of ancient flat bread. One common type of oven, still used in Syria, is a cylindrical structure made of mortar. At the bottom of the structure, a wood fire heats the mortar. The dough is placed on the hot surface to bake. When finished, it is lifted off.

Except for certain ceremonies, bread was made with yeast, or more precisely, leaven. The concept of leaven is less familiar today, when pure dehydrated yeast is used. In Bible times, a bit of the dough was put aside before baking a batch of bread to be used as the "starter" for the next batch, as with sourdough starter. This practice was common; it was referred to in Jesus's teaching. Substituting "yeast" for leaven in modern translations (such as NLT) can confuse the present-day reader, who might envision pure, dehydrated yeast. Rather, the ancient leaven was a mixture of yeast and dough.

Bread was used in some of the Levitical offerings. "Consecrated bread" was placed each week on the golden table by the lamp stand in the tabernacle and Temple, a reminder that bread was associated with God's provision (Exodus 29). Other offerings required a diversity of bread: "And one loaf of bread, and one cake of oiled bread, and one wafer, out of the basket of unleavened bread that is before Jehovah" (Exodus 29:23, ASV). In summary, bread was widely used in the sacrifices.

Wheat flour was produced by grinding in hand mills or with querns. Querns are usually large stones in which a shallow trough has been ground or worn. Grain is put in the trough and ground, using a smaller stone that fits into the groove. Both types of grinding were practiced in the ancient Middle East.

Hand mills were made from two flat stones, circular in shape and of equal size. In the center of the stone was a hole through which a wooden or iron shaft could be placed to turn the upper stone while the lower stone remained stationary. Grain was fed into the mill through an additional hole in the upper stone. Shallow grooves were cut into the stones so that when the upper stone was turned, the grain was ground, and was forced out through the grooves.

Such hand mills were as common in ancient households as microwave ovens are today. Family dependence on the mill is evident in a verse where the upper part of a hand mill could not be taken as security: "No one may take a mill or a millstone in pledge; that would be to take life itself in pledge" (Deuteronomy 24:6, NJB). In another verse, the upper stone of a hand mill was used as a lethal weapon: "So Abimelech came to the tower and fought against it, and approached the entrance of the tower to burn it with fire. But a certain woman threw an upper millstone on Abimelech's head, crushing his skull" (Judges 9:52–53, NASB).

B READ AND FLOUR MAY BE well-known Bible images, but beer is not, though it was an ingredient in at least one of the Levitical offerings: "The Drink-Offering that goes with it is a quart of strong beer with each lamb. Pour out the Drink-Offering before God in the Sanctuary" (Numbers 28:7, MSG). Beer is mentioned in at least nine verses, though usually not with a positive connotation: "It is not for kings, O Lemuel—not for kings to drink wine, not for rulers to crave beer, lest they drink and forget what the law decrees, and deprive all the oppressed of their rights. Give beer to those who are perishing, wine to those who are in anguish; let them drink and forget their poverty and remember their misery no more" (Proverbs 31:4–7, NIV).

Beer production in the ancient Middle East and Egypt is well documented. Delwen Samuel has given us insight into ancient baking and brewing (Nesbitt and Samuel 1996, Samuel 2000). With scanning electron microscopy of starch grains and yeast cells, Samuel showed that Egyptians used a malting process in their beer. Sieves, frequently pictured in tombs, were apparently used to remove the large quantities of chaff in the brew. Barley was the main ingredient in beer, although wheat was also used to a lesser extent (Samuel 2000). Since the same grains were grown in Canaan, it seems likely that the same process was used.

L IKE BEER, ROASTED GRAIN, or "parched corn" as translated in KJV, is a lesser known Bible wheat product found only in Leviticus 23:14; Joshua 5:11; Ruth 2:14; I Samuel 17:17; and I Samuel 25:18. Could roasted grain be *frikeh*? Throughout modern-day northern Syria, *frikeh* is a traditional preparation of green wheat. *Frikeh* is made from wheat with green heads. Dried for at least two hours after cutting, the wheat is then burned until the chaff is black and the tip of the grain is charred. Barley is harvested at the same time as *frikeh* production, so barley straw was readily available as a fuel for a cool fire. As soon as the charred green wheat is cool enough to handle, the grains are removed from the heads for tasting. The soft, green grains are chewy, slightly sweet, with a desirable smoky taste. When fresh, *frikeh* can be cooked with meat, like rice. It is usually dried, however, and cracked, because cracking shortens the cooking time. *Frikeh* is ideally dried in the shade to avoid bleaching the green grains. Traditionally, durum wheat is used to make *frikeh*, but bread wheat is also used. In Bible days, emmer was used since it was grown almost exclusively (Musselman and Mouslem 2001).

Could *frikeh* be the roasted or parched grain mentioned in the Bible? In the widely used Van Dyck edition of the Arabic Bible (1865), parched corn (KJV) or roasted grain (NIV) is translated *frikeh* in the six verses where it occurs. In the Syriac text, *froka*, a cognate of *frikeh*, is used. In Hebrew, the word is *kawlee*, which is derived from a word meaning "to scorch" or "to parch."

Frikeh is a good candidate for roasted grain because of its association with the barley harvest and its use as a dried provision. The suggestion that *kawlee* is sorghum has little basis (Moldenke and Moldenke 1952). In Ruth, roasted corn was eaten at the barley harvest, which is when *frikeh* is prepared; this coincides well with the timing of modern production. In the references in I and II Samuel, roasted grain is associated with other dried foods (beans, raisins) that can be readily transported.

The word in Joshua 5:11 is different. The New Living Translation renders this as "roasted grain" but notes that it was "some of the produce of the land." In other words, this was not grain that had been brought across the Jordan. Could this be fresh *frikeh*?

BIBLE READERS MAY seldom think of straw as being valuable to farmers in ancient Israel. But the straw from wheat can be as valuable as the grain under some circumstances (Murray 2000). As in the days of the Pharaohs (Exodus 5:10–13), straw is still important for brick making in rural Mesopotamia and elsewhere. Straw from either wheat or barley is mixed with mud and put into wooden forms to make bricks. Wheat straw is more commonly used because barley straw is more valuable as fodder. Humble dwellings are made from sun-baked bricks. Fire-baked bricks are more durable and were used to make some of the buildings in the Fertile Crescent that still stand. Straw is also mixed with the mortar of the mud houses characteristic of the northern Fertile Crescent. Chaff was widely used as a temper in brick making in ancient Egypt (Kemp 2000).

Less enduring than bricks, baskets and mats were necessary every-

Frikeh, roasted green wheat, drying on sidewalks in Aleppo, Syria. After drying, the grain is cracked and sold.

day items and could be made from straw. Making baskets from cereal straw has almost vanished from the Middle East today, with the advent of synthetic materials. There are no explicit references to making baskets in the Bible, but in ancient days long-stemmed wheat stalks were no doubt valued for this purpose. And straw, though without specific references, was likely used in construction, to make roofs of temporary houses. This wattle-and-daub roof construction with straw as one of the constituents was used as recently as the past century.

Sometimes used for fodder, straw of wheat was more frequently used as bedding for animals in the Bible. So it was an important item to have on hand for animal care, as when the servant of Abraham arrives to seek a bride for Isaac: "So the man [Abraham's servant] went to the house, and the camels were unloaded. Straw and fodder were brought for the camels, and water for him and his men to wash their feet" (Genesis 24:32, NIV). Linked with chaff and easily burned, straw is mentioned by the Apostle Paul as an image of poor spiritual investment: "On this foundation, different people may build in gold, silver, jewels, wood, hay or straw but each person's handiwork will be shown for what it is. The Day which dawns in fire will make it clear and the fire itself will test the quality of each person's work" (I Corinthians 3:12–13, NJB).

The most humble wheat product, chaff, is the only part of the wheat that has little or no value. In the approximately twenty references in the Bible, chaff always refers to something worthless and of little weight, which can easily be carried before the wind. The following example is perhaps the best known: "Blessed is the man who does not walk in the counsel of the wicked or stand in the way of sinners or sit in the seat of mockers. But his delight is in the law of the Lord, and on his law he meditates day and night. He is like a tree planted by streams of water, which yields its fruit in season and whose leaf does not wither. Whatever he does prospers. Not so the wicked! They are like chaff that the wind blows away" (Psalm 1:1–4, NIV).

In contrast to its scriptural imagery, cereal chaff is now of exceptional value to archeobotanists. It contains microscopic inclusions of silicon called phytoliths. Phytoliths are distinctive for each species. By examining the phytoliths from chaff from archaeological sites, it is possible to determine which plants were used.

The importance of wheat in the cultures of the Middle East cannot be overemphasized. Wheat originated in that region, and its domestication is one of the epochal events in the history of human civilization.

Manufacturing sun-dried bricks in Morocco with straw from wheat. Sun-dried bricks are a low-cost building material, without the expense of firing the bricks.

Wild Greens

Salt glands are present on the undersurface of the saltbush leaf. In March, International Center for Agricultural Research in the Dry Areas, Tel Hadya, Syria.

W HAT DO WILD GREENS AND mallow have in common? Numerous plants in different parts of the world provide "wild greens." And as for mallows, this common name is usually associated with members of the genus *Hibiscus*. So what is this plant and why is it translated in such disparate ways? The only reference is in Job, in a discourse that is a tirade on Job's part, impugning those whom he views as judging them. Put another way, he considers these coarse vagabonds with little credibility or, in his own words, "a base and nameless brood" (Job 30:8, NIV). Strong language for men who apparently know how to survive in nature.

Many plants have edible foliage but few are large enough to provide a meaningful amount of food. One of these is a common desert shrub translated "mallow" (in KJV)—not to be confused with a group of wetland plants by that common name—and translated "salt herbs" in NIV: "Haggard from want and hunger, they roamed the parched land in desolate wastelands at night. In the brush they gathered salt herbs, and their food was the root of the broom tree" (Job 30:3–4, NIV).

The solitary reference to wild greens was translated from the Hebrew *malluach*, hence the inappropriate translation "mallow," in this verse. The much-branched, gray-green shrub is often associated with broom, the desert plant. The precise identity of this food source is not clear, but it is likely *Atriplex halimus*, a desert plant sometimes referred to as saltbush, which can tolerate high levels of salinity. I have eaten the leaves, which possess salt secreting glands, and I found them pleasant. I like mallow slightly steamed, and it is edible raw. The plant, however, is not favored for fodder. The modern translation *The Message* renders *malluach* as "chewing on old bones and licking old tin cans," eviscerating any botanical meaning from the text.

The semiarid regions of the Middle East provide few edible plant resources. The plant translated as "wild greens" (or mallow) is one of them.

Atriplex halimus is widely planted
to improve land in steppe regions
where vegetation has been heavily
overgrazed. In March, International
Center for Agricultural Research
in the Dry Areas, Tel Hadya, Syria.

Willow

Leaves and branches of willow in northern Israel along the Jordan River.

WEEPING WILLOW IS A MISNO-mer for any tree in the Bible and in fact is not even native to western Asia. Consider this verse: "By the rivers of Babylon, there we sat down and wept, when we remembered Zion. Upon the willows in the midst of it we hung our harps" (Psalm 137:1–2, NASB). The "willows" of Babylon are probably not true willows but rather a kind of poplar, *Populus euphratica*.

There are several species of true willow in the Middle East; two of the more common are *Salix acmophylla* and *S. alba*. The Bible does not indicate which species are meant. Willows are common along permanent watercourses and form dense thickets along the banks of the Jordan River, especially at its upper reaches. These denizens of stream banks are mentioned in only four places: "On the first day [of the Feast of Shelters] you will take choice fruit, palm branches, boughs of leafy trees and flowering shrubs from the river bank, and for seven days enjoy yourselves before Yahweh your God" (Leviticus 23:40, NJB); "The leaves of the lotus give him shade the willows by the stream shelter him" (Job 40:22, NJB); "That is why they are carrying what they could save of their stores across the Ravine of the Willows [or poplars]" (Isaiah 15:7, NJB); and, "They will spring up among the grass, like willows on the banks of a stream" (Isaiah 44:4, NJB).

The willow is a much-branched shrub or small tree with narrow, pointed leaves that are lighter green on the bottom surface. Each shrub

Willows along the
upper reaches of the
Jordan River, Israel.

is unisexual and the flowers are minute and borne in the spring. The seeds are equipped with hairs that enable them to float through the air and ensure their dispersal. For eons, the bark of the willow has been used as a medicine; it is from willow bark that aspirin was first extracted.

The wood of willow is soft and not very durable. But it was used in Bible days for bowls, other utensils, and some construction (Gale et al. 2000). While the wood is considered poor quality, the narrow stems, or withes (also spelled withs), are still used to make baskets and may have been used by Delilah to bind Samson (Judges 16:7–9). A traditional use of willow wood in Syria is for crafting a form for darning clothing: the wood is cut into an egg-shaped structure that fits into a sock and easily absorbs darning needle jabs.

Wormwood

WORMWOOD IS ENIGMATIC; WE cannot with certainty name the plant indicated by the Hebrew *la'anah* in seven Bible verses. But since *la'anah* is linked with gall in two instances, a different plant than wormwood could be intended. As implied in the verses, the plant should be bitter, be used for making a decoction (prepared by boiling the plant extract), and be drunk without poisoning (Jeremiah 9:15, 23:15).

Developing flowers on the wormwood shrub. At this stage, the plant is collected for medicinal use.

In the New Testament, wormwood is found only in Revelation 8:11, where a star is called Wormwood. The Greek word is *apsinthos*, which implies a bitter or poisonous plant. This verse states that some who drank of the wormwood died, suggesting that it is toxic. Of course, we must take into account the symbolic imagery of Revelation before assigning a botanical name to the wormwood.

What native plant in the Middle East conforms to the characteristics of wormwood in the Bible? Most studies on Bible plants (for example, Harrison 1966) implicate a compact, woody shrub in the sunflower family, *Artemisia herba-alba*, known in English as wormwood. Wormwood has been known as a medicine since ancient times. A decoction of the leaves is used to cure intestinal worms, hence the common name. But today the plant is seldom used for its antihelminthic property.

Heavily grazed wormwood
shrub in July, near Wadi
Mousa, southern Jordan.

A flavoring for alcoholic drinks is made from wormwood, which is known in English as absinthe, directly derived from the Greek word used in the New Testament. It is also known as "bitters." Absinthe has an intensely bitter taste, which may add to its desirability as a medicine under the philosophy that anything that tastes that bad must be good for you.

Wormwood is the dominant plant in vast areas of steppe in the Middle East. The silvery green leaves of this shrub give it a distinctive appearance when the rest of the vegetation is dry. Unlike many members of the native flora, the wormwood plant flowers in the middle of the summer. In addition to its medicinal value, it is a valuable fodder plant, and in some areas wormwood is severely overgrazed.

References

Andrews, A. C. 1958. The mints of the Greeks and Romans and their condimentary uses. *Osiris* 13: 127–149.

Ataman, K. 1999. Threshing sledges and archeology. In P. C. Anderson, ed. *Prehistory of Agriculture: New Experimental and Ethnographic Approaches*, Monograph 40. Los Angeles: University of California–Los Angeles, Institute of Archeology. 211–222.

Baruah, J. N., R. K. Mathur, S. M. Jain, and J. C. S. Kataky. 1982. Agar wood *Aquilaria agallaocha*, agar oil, fragment resinous wood, use as incense [sic], India. In C. K. Atal and B. M. Kapur, eds. *Cultivation and Utilization of Aromatic Plants*. Jammu-Tawi, India: Regional Research Lab. 662–667.

Baumann, H. 1993. *The Greek Plant World in Myth, Art, and Literature*. Trans. W. T. and E. R. Stearn. Portland, Oregon: Timber Press.

Biger, G., and N. Liphschitz. 1991. The recent distribution of *Pinus brutia*: A reassessment based on dendroarchaeological and dendrohistorical evidence from Israel. *The Holocene* 1(2): 157–161.

Bikai, P. M. 1991. *The Cedar of Lebanon: Archaeological and Dendrochronological Perspectives*. PhD dissertation. Berkeley: University of California.

Brun, J. P. 2000. The production of perfumes in antiquity: The cases of Delos and Paestum. *American Journal of Archaeology* 104(2): 277–308.

Buckley, S. A., and R. F. Evershed. 2001. Organic chemistry of embalming agents in Pharaonic and Graeco-Roman mummies. *Nature* 413: 837–841.

Buhagiar, J., M. T. Camilleri Podestà, P. L. Cioni, G. Flamini, and I. Morelli. 2000. Essential oil composition of different parts of *Tetraclinis articulata*. *Journal of Essential Oils Research* 12: 29–32.

Calkin, R. R. and J. S. Jellinek. 1994. *Perfumery: Practices and Principles*. New York: Wiley-Interscience.

Threshing floor for lentils east of Bethlehem. The same threshing floor is used for barley, which is harvested at about the same time.

Chaudhary, S. A. 2001. Rhamnaceae. In S. A. Chaudhary, ed. *Flora of the Kingdom of Saudi Arabia*. Vol. II (1). Riyadh: National Agriculture and Water Research Center. 396–410.

Colombini, M. P., F. Modugno, F. Silvano, and M. Onor. 2000. Characterization of the balm of an Egyptian mummy from the seventh century BC. *Studies in Conservation* 45: 19–29.

Dafni, A. 2003. Why are rags tied to the sacred trees of the holy land? *Economic Botany* 56(4): 315–327.

Danin, A. 1979. The Atlantic pistachio, largest of Israel's trees. *Israel: Land and Nature* 5(3): 114–116.

Danne, A., F. Peterett, and A. Nahrstedt. 1993. Proanthocyanidins from *Cistus incanus*. *Phytochemistry* 34(4): 1129–1133.

Demetzos, C., B. Stahl, T. Anastassaki, M. Gazouli, L. S. Tzouvelekis, and M. Rallis. 1999. Chemical analysis and antimicrobial activity of the resin ladano, of its essential oil and of the isolated compounds. *Planta Medica* 65: 76–78.

Demetzos, C., H. Katerinopoulos, A. Kouvarakis, N. Stratigakis, A. Loukis, C. Ekonomakis, V. Spiliotis, and J. Tsanknis. 1997. Composition and antimicrobial activity of the essential oil of *Cistus creticus*. subsp. *eriocephalus*. *Planta Medica* 63: 477–479.

de Vartavan, C. Amorós, and V. A. Amorós. 1997. *Codex of Ancient Egyptian Plant Remains*. London: Triade Exploration.

Diederichsen, A., and K. Hamer. 2003. The infraspecific taxa of coriander (*Coriandrum sativum* L.). *Genetic Resources and Crop Evolution* 50: 33–63.

Dinsmore, J. 1932. *Revision of Post's Flora of Syria, Palestine, and Sinai from the Taurus to Ras Muhammad and from the Mediterranean Sea to the Syrian Desert*. Beirut: American Press.

Dixon, D. M. 1974. Timber in ancient Egypt. *Commonwealth Forest Review* 53: 205–209.

Dolara, P., C .Luceri, D. Ghelardini, C. Monserrat, S. Aiolli, F. Luceri, M. Lodovici, S. Menichetti, and M. N. Romanelli. 1996. Analgesic effects of myrrh. *Nature* 379: 29.

el Bahri, S., M. Djegham, and H. Bellil. 1999. *Retama raetam* W [sic]: A poisonous plant of North Africa. *Veterinary and human toxicology* 41(1): 33–35.

Ertug, F. 1998. Plant-gathering versus plant domestication: An ethnobotanical focus on leafy plants. In Damania, A. B., J. Valkoun, G. Willcox, and C. O. Qualset, eds. *The Origins of Agriculture and Crop Domestication*.

Aleppo, Syria: International Center for Agricultural Research in the Dry Areas. 218–223.

Farjon, J. 2005. *A Monograph of Cupressaceae and Sciadopitys*. Kew: Royal Botanic Gardens.

Farooqi, M. I. H. 2001. *Medicinal Plants in the Traditions of Prophet Muhammad*. 2nd ed. Lucknow: Sidrah Publishers.

Farooqi, M. I. H. 2003. *Plants of the Qur'an*. Lucknow: Sidrah Publishers.

Fernandes-Carlos, T., J. Riondel, D. Glise, P. Guiraud, and A. Favier. 1997. Modulation of natural killer cell functional activity in athymic mice by beta-carotene, oestrone, and their assocation. *Anticancer Research* 17(4a): 2523–2528.

Fernández, J. A., and F. Abdullaev, eds. 2004. International Symposium on Saffron Biology and Biotechnology. Compact disc. *ISHS Acta Horticulturae* 650.

Flamini, G., A. Bader, P. L. Cioni, A. Katbeh-Bader, and I. Morelli. 2004. Composition of the essential oil, leaves, galls, and ripe and unripe fruits of Jordanian *Pistacia terebinthus* var. *palaestina* Boiss. *Journal of Agricultural and Food Chemistry* 52: 572–576.

Fleisher, A., and Z. Fleisher. 1988. Identification of biblical hyssop and origin of the traditional use of oregano-group herbs in the Mediterranean region. *Economic Botany* 42(2): 232–241.

Fleisher, A., and Z. Fleisher. 1994. The fragrance of biblical mandrake. *Economic Botany* 48(3): 243–251.

Forster, E. S. 1952. Trees and plants in the Greek tragic writers. *Greece & Rome* 21(62): 57–63.

Foster, B. O. 1899. Notes on the symbolism of the apple in classical antiquity. *Harvard Studies in Classical Philology* 10: 39–55.

Gale, R., P. Gasson, F. N. Hepper, and G. Killen. 2000. Wood. In P. T. Nicholson and I. Shaw, eds. *Ancient Egyptian Materials and Technology*. Cambridge, UK: Cambridge University Press. 334–371.

Galil, J. 1968. An ancient technique for ripening sycomore fruit in East Mediterranean countries. *Economic Botany* 22: 178–190.

Galil, J. 1977. On the origin of the sycomore fig (*Ficus sycomorus*) in the Middle East. *Gardens' Bulletin, Singapore* 29: 191–205.

Green, P. S. 2002. A revision of *Olea* L. *Kew Bulletin* 57(1): 91–140.

Greenfield, J. C., and M. Mayrhofer. 1967. The "algumm" / "almuggim" problem reexamined. *Supplements to Vetus Testamentum* 6: 83–89.

Greppin, J. A. C. 1988. The various aloes in ancient times. *Journal of Indo-European Studies* 16(1–2): 33–48.

Greppin, J. A. C. 1995. Comments on early Armenian knowledge of botany as revealed in the geography of Ananias of Shirak. *Journal of the American Oriental Society* 115(4): 679–684.

Hammouda, F. M., A. M. Rizk, M. M. El-Missiry, H. A. Ghaleb, M. K, Madkour, A. E. Pohland, and G. Wood. 1988. Poisonous plants contaminating edible ones and toxic substances in plant foods. IV: Phytochemistry and toxicity of *Lolium temulentum. International Journal of Crude Drug Research* 26: 240–245.

Harrison, R. K. 1956. The mandrake and the ancient world. *The Evangelical Quarterly* 28(2): 87–92.

Harrison, R. K. 1966. *Healing Herbs of the Bible.* Leiden: E. J. Brill.

Hepper, F. N. 1993. *Baker Encyclopedia of Bible Plants: Flowers and Trees, Fruits and Vegetables, Ecology.* Grand Rapids: Baker Book House.

Hillman, G. 1981. Traditional husbandry and processing of archaic cereals in recent times: The operations, products, and equipment which might feature in Sumerian Texts. Part I: The glume wheats. *Bulletin on Sumerian Agriculture* I: 114–142.

Homan, M. M. 2002. *To your Tents, O Israel! The Terminology, Function, Form, and Symbolism of Tents in the Hebrew Bible and the Ancient Near East.* Leiden: Brill.

Hughes, J. D. 1983. How the ancients viewed deforestation. *Journal of Field Archaeology* 10(4): 435–445.

Janick, J., and H. S. Paris. 2006. The cucurbit images (1515–1518) of the Villa Farnesina, Rome. *Annals of Botany* 97: 165–176.

Jones, H., and L. Mann. 1963. *Onions and Their Allies.* New York: Inter-Science Publishers.

Juniper, B. E., and D. J. Mabberley. 2006. *The Story of the Apple.* Portland, Oregon: Timber Press.

Kadry, A., and S. Kamel. 1959. Morphological studies in *Allium kurrat* Schweinf., *A. porrum* L., and their hybrid. *Svenska Botaniska Tidskrift* 53(2): 187–199.

Kafi, M., A. Koocheki, M. H. Rashed, M. Nassiri, eds. 2006. *Saffron (*Crocus sativus*) Production and Processing.* Enfield, New Hampshire: Science Publishers.

Kaiser, J. 1997. Thuya burl: The underground treasure. *Wood & Wood Products* 102(5): 1–4.

Kaplan, D., D. Pevzner, M. Galilee, and M Gutman. 1995. Traditional selective harvesting effects on occurrence and reproductive growth of *Gundelia tournefortii* in Israel grasslands. *Israel Journal of Plant Sciences* 43: 163–166.

Kemp, B. 2000. Soil (including mud-brick architecture). In P. T. Nicholson and I. Shaw, eds. *Ancient Egyptian Materials and Technology*. Cambridge: Cambridge University Press. 78–103.

Kevan, P. G., and T. Ebert. 2005. Can almond nectar & pollen poison honey bees? *American Bee Journal* 145(6): 507–509.

Khafagi, I., A. Zakaria, A. Dewedar, and K. el-Zahdany. 2006. A voyage in the world of plants as mentioned in the holy Quran. *International Journal of Botany* 2(3): 242–251.

Langenheim, J. H. 2003. *Plant Resins: Chemistry, Evolution, Ecology, and Ethnobotany*. Portland, Oregon: Timber Press.

Larsen, H. O. 2005. Impact of replanting on regeneration of the medicinal plant *Nardostachys grandiflora* DC. (Valerianaceae). *Economic Botany* 59(3): 213–220.

le Strange, G., transl. 1896. Description of Syria, including Palestine. In *The Library of the Palestine Pilgrims' Text Society*. Vol. III. 1971 ed. New York: AMS Press.

Leung, A. Y., and S. Foster. 1996. *Encyclopedia of Common Natural Ingredients Used in Food, Drugs, and Cosmetics*. 2nd ed. New York: Wiley-Interscience.

Levey, M. 1954. The early history of detergent substances: A chapter in Babylonian chemistry. *Journal of Chemical Education* 521–524.

Lev-Yadun, S. 1992. The origin of the cedar beams from Al-Aqsa Mosque: Botanical, historical, and archaeological evidence. *Levant* 24: 201–208.

Liphschitz, N., and G. Biger. 2001. Past distribution of Aleppo pine (*Pinus halepensis*) in the mountains of Israel (Palestine). *The Holocene* 11(4): 427–436.

Liphschitz, N., S. Lev-Yadun, and Y. Waisel. 1981. Dendroarchaeological investigations in Israel (Masada). *Israel Exploration Society* 31: 230–234.

Löw, I. 1967. *Die Flora der Juden*. Vol. I-IV. Reprint of 1928 ed. Hildesheim: Georg Olms.

Madmon, A., G. Schiller, Y. Moshe, G. Tsabary, Z. Mendel, and J. Riov. 2003. Controlled and open pollination between *Pinus brutia* (Ten.) [sic] and *Pinus halepensis* (Mill.) [sic] in Israel and hybrid performance. *Israel Journal of Plant Sciences* 51: 213–222.

Mansour, S., M. Al-Said, M. Tariq, M. A. Al-Yahya, S. Rafatullah, O.

T. Ginnawi, and A. M. Ageel. 1990. Studies on *Ruta chalepensis*, an ancient medicinal herb still used in traditional medicine. *Journal of Ethnopharmacology* 28: 305–312.

Mathew, B. 1996. *A Review of* Allium *sect.* Allium. Kew: Royal Botanic Gardens.

May, Herbert G., ed. 1984. *Oxford Bible Atlas*, 3rd ed., rev. by John Day. Oxford: Oxford University Press.

Meiggs, R. 1982. *Trees and Timber in the Ancient Mediterranean World*. Oxford: University Press.

Metcalfe, D. J. 2005. Biological flora of the British Isles. *Hedera helix* L. *Journal of Ecology* 93: 632–648.

Miller, J. I. 1969. *The Spice Trade of the Roman Empire*. Oxford: Clarendon.

Moldenke, H. N., and A. L. Moldenke. 1952. *Plants of the Bible*. Chronica Botanica. New York: Ronald Press.

Motley, T. J. 1994. The ethnobotany of sweet flag, *Acorus calamus* (Araceae). *Economic Botany* 48(4): 397–412.

Murray, M. A. 2000. Fruits, vegetables, pulses, and condiments. In P. T. Nicholson and I. Shaw, eds. *Ancient Egyptian Materials and Technology*. Cambridge: Cambridge University Press. 609–655.

Murray, M. A. 2000a. Cereal production and processing. In P. T. Nicholson and I. Shaw, eds. *Ancient Egyptian Materials and Technology*. Cambridge: Cambridge University Press. 505–536.

Musselman, L. J. 1999. Solomon's plant life. Plant lore and image in the Solomonic writings. *Perspectives on Science and Christian Faith* 51(10): 1–8.

Musselman, L. J. 2000. *Jordan in Bloom: Wildflowers of the Holy Land*. Illus. by Dasha Fomicheva. Amman: Jordan River Foundation.

Musselman, L. J. 2001. *Zawan* and tares in the Bible. *Economic Botany* 54(4): 537–542.

Musselman, L. J. 2003. Is *Allium kurrat* the leek of the Bible? *Economic Botany* 56(4): 399–400.

Musselman, L. J. 2003a. Trees in the Qu'ran and the Bible. *Unasylva* 213(54): 45–52.

Musselman, L. J. 2006. The botanical activities of George Edward Post (1838–1909). *Archives of Natural History* 33(2). 282–301.

Musselman, L. J., and H. P. Medema. 1993. *Laat de Aarde het u Vertellen: De zwijgende maar machtige boodschape von planten in het land van de Bijbel*. Vaassen, Netherlands: Medema.

Musselman, L.J., and H. P. Medema. 1993a. *Van U is ook de Aarde: De zwijgende maarmachtige boodschap von planten in het heiligdom.* Vaassen, Netherlands: Medema.

Musselman, L. J., and A. B. Mouslem. 2001. *Frikeh*, roasted green wheat. *Economic Botany* 55(2): 187–189.

Ne'eman, G., S. Goubitz, and R. Nathan. 2004. Reproductive traits of *Pinus halepensis* in the light of fire: A critical review. *Plant Ecology* 171: 69–79.

Nesbitt, M., and D. Samuel. 1996. In Padulosi, S., K. Hammer, and J. Heller, eds. Hulled Wheats: Promoting the conservation and use of underutilized and neglected crops. 4. *Proceedings of the First International Workshop on Hulled Wheats.* Rome: International Plant Genetic Resources Institute. 41–100.

Nicholson, P. T., and I. Shaw, eds. 2000. *Ancient Egyptian Materials and Technology.* Cambridge: Cambridge University Press.

O'Connell, R. H. 1991. Proverbs VII: 16–17: A case of fatal deception and "Woman and the window" type-scene. *Vetus Testamentum* 41(2): 235–241.

Oomah, B. D. 2001. Flaxseed as a functional food source. *Journal of the Sciences of Food and Agriculture* 81: 889–894.

Patrich, J., and B. Arubas. 1989. A juglet containing balsam oil (?) from a cave near Qumran. *Israel Exploration Journal* 39: 43–59.

Piccirillo, M. 1992. *The Mosaics of Jordan.* Amman, Jordan: American Center of Oriental Research.

Pojanagaroon, S., and C. Kaewrak. 2005. Mechanical methods to stimulate aloes wood formation in *Aquilaria crassna* Pierre ex H. Lec. (kritsana) trees. *Acta Horticulturae* 676: 161–166.

Post, G. E. 1896. *Flora of Syria, Palestine and Sinai from the Tauras to Ras Muhammad and from the Mediterranean Sea to the Syrian Desert.* Beirut: Syrian Protestant College.

Post, G. E. 1901. Algum trees, almug trees. In J. Hastings, ed. *A Dictionary of the Bible Dealing with its Language, Literature, and Contents Including the Biblical Theology.* Vol. I. New York: Scribners. 63.

Post, G. E. 1901b. Mustard. In J. Hastings, ed. *A Dictionary of the Bible Dealing with its Language, Literature, and Contents Including the Biblical Theology.* Vol. III. New York: Scribners. 462.

Post, G. E. 1901c. Myrtle. In J. Hastings, ed. *A Dictionary of the Bible Dealing with its Language, Literature, and Contents Including the Biblical Theology.* Vol. III. New York: Scribners. 465.

Post, G. E. 1903. Galbanum. In J. Hastings, J., ed. *A Dictionary of the Bible Dealing with its Language, Literature, and Contents Including the Biblical Theology.* Vol. II. New York: Scribners. 98.

Rackham, H., transl. 2000. *Pliny Natural History Books XII-XVI.* Cambridge: Harvard University Press. Loeb Classical Library. IV(XIII).

Ross, E. 1995. Touba: A spiritual metropolis in the modern world. *Canadian Journal of African Studies* 29(2): 222–259.

Samuel, D. 2000. Brewing and baking. In P. T. Nicholson and I. Shaw, eds. *Ancient Egyptian Materials and Technology.* Cambridge: Cambridge University Press. 537–576.

Schoff, W. H. 1922. Aloes. *Journal of the American Oriental Society* 42: 171–195.

Seow, C. L. 1999. Qohelet's eschalotological poem. *Journal of Biblical Literature* 118(2): 209–234.

Serpico, M. 2000. Resins, amber, and bitumen. In P. T. Nicholson and I. Shaw, eds. *Ancient Egyptian Materials and Technology.* Cambridge: Cambridge University Press. 430–474.

Simpson, B. B., and M. C. Ogorzaly. 2000. *Economic Botany: Plants in Our World.* 3rd ed. New York: McGraw-Hill.

Sozzi, G. O. 2001. Caper bush: Botany and horticulture. *Horticulture Reviews* 27: 125–188.

Täckhom, V., and M. Drar. 1954. *Flora of Egypt.* Vol. III. *Allium* in Ancient Egypt. Cairo: Cairo University Press. 93–106.

Thompson, R. C. 1937. Assyrian prescriptions for the head (concluded). *American Journal of Semitic Languages and Literatures* 54(1 / 4): 12–40.

Thulin, M., and P. Claeson. 1991. The botanical origin of scented myrrh (*bissabol* or *habak hadi*). *Economic Botany* 45(4): 487–494.

Todd, J. E. 1886. The caper-berry (Eccles. Xii 5). *Journal of the Society of Biblical Literature and Exegesis* 16(6): 13–26.

Trapp, J. B. 1958. The owl's ivy and the poet's bays: An enquiry into poetic garlands. *Journal of the Warburg and Courtauld Institutes* 21(3 / 4): 227–255.

Trever, J. C. 1959. The flora of the Bible and biblical scholarship. *Journal of Bible and Religion* 27(1): 45–49.

Troccoli, A., and P. Codianni. 2005. Appropriate seeding rate for einkorn, emmer, and spelt grown under rainfed condition in southern Italy. *European Journal of Agronomy* 22: 293–300.

United Bible Societies. 1980. *Helps for Translators: Fauna and Flora of the Bible*. New York: United Bible Societies.

Vaughan, J. G., and J. S. Hemingway. 1959. The utilization of mustards. *Economic Botany* 13(2): 196–204.

Vogelsang-Eastwood, G. 2000. Textiles. In P. T. Nicholson and I. Shaw, eds. *Ancient Egyptian Materials and Technology*. Cambridge: Cambridge University Press. 268–298.

Watkins, C. 1978. Let us now praise famous grains. *Proceedings of the American Philosophical Society* 122(1): 9–17.

Welborn, M. C. 1932. The errors of the doctors, according to Friar Roger Bacon of the Minor Order. *Isis* 18(1): 26–62.

Wendrich, W. Z. 2000. Basketry. In P. T. Nicholson and I. Shaw, eds. *Ancient Egyptian Materials and Technology*. Cambridge: Cambridge University Press. 254–267.

Whiston, W., n.d.. *The Works of Flavius Josephus, The Learned and Authentic Jewish Historian and Celebrated Warrior*. Philadelphia: Winston Company.

Worrell, W. H. 1947. Note on modern Coptic ink. *Isis* 37(3 / 4): 149–150.

Yazicioğlu, T., A. Karaali, and J. Gőkçen. 1978. *Cephalaria syriaca* seed oil. *Journal of the American Oil Chemist's Society* 4: 412–415.

Yesilada E., I. Gurbuz, and H. Shibata. 1999. Screening of Turkish anti-ulcerogenic folk remedies for anti-*Helicobacter pylori* activity. *Journal of Ethnopharmacology* 66(3): 289–93.

Zaleman, L. 1980. Piercing the darkness at *bôqêr* (Amos VII: 14). *Vetus Testamentum* 30(2): 252–253.

Zohary, M. 1973. *Geobotanical Foundations of the Middle East*. Vols. I and II. Stuttgart: Gustav Fischer Verlag.

Zohary, M. 1982. *Plants of the Bible*. Cambridge: Cambridge University Press.

Zohary, D., and M. Hopf. 2000. *Domestication of Plants in the Old World: The Origin and Spread of Cultivated Plants in West Asia, Europe, and the Nile Valley*. 3rd ed. Oxford: Clarendon Press.

Index to Verses in the Bible and the Quran

General Index